PERSPECTIVES ON WAR AND PEACE
IN CENTRAL AMERICA

PERSPECTIVES ON WAR AND PEACE
IN CENTRAL AMERICA

edited by

Sung Ho Kim and Thomas W. Walker

Ohio University Center for International Studies
Monographs in International Studies

Latin America Series Number 19
Athens, Ohio 1992

Library of Congress Cataloging-in-Publication Data

Perspectives on war and peace in Central America / edited by
Sung Ho Kim and Thomas W. Walker.
    p.   cm. – (Monographs in international studies. Latin
America series ; no. 19)
    Papers presented during a symposium, held at Ohio
University on Nov. 4–5, 1988.
    ISBN 0-89680-172-1
    1. Central America–Foreign relations–1979-
–Congresses.   2. Central America–Politics and
government–1979- –Congresses. 3. Central America–
Foreign relations–United States–Congresses. 4. United
States–Foreign relations–Central America–Congresses.
5. Procedure to establish Steady and Long-Standing Peace
in Central America (1987) –Congresses.   I. Kim, Sung-ho.
II. Walker, Thomas W.   III. Ohio University. Center for
International studies.   IV. Series.
F1439.5.P48   1992
327.728—dc20   92-8970
                                                            CIP

CONTENTS

FOREWORD

This volume is a historical document designed to present the edited papers or statements of eleven prominent people who met for a symposium at Ohio University on 4 and 5 November 1988 to present their "Perspectives on War and Peace in Central America." As Sung Ho Kim notes in the first chapter, that point in time was a crucial juncture in the search for peace in the region. The Arias Peace Agreement had been signed a little over a year earlier and much progress towards implementing that accord had been made in the ensuing period. Nevertheless, the United States, pursuing its "privilege of power," was continuing to block any solution to the conflicts which would leave the Sandinistas in office in Nicaragua.

The symposium was designed to provide a forum for the airing of diverse perspectives on the Central American problem. These would include not only opposing political viewpoints but also a variety of professional and national outlooks. The symposium began on the morning of 4 November with an exchange of views between prominent U.S. scholars. Political scientist Howard Wiarda of the American Enterprise Institute and the University of Massachusetts gave a conservative interpretation; historian Walter LaFeber of Cornell University countered with a liberal perspective.

In the afternoon, Francesc Vendrell, a Catalan involved in observing the peace process through his official role as a United Nations representative, gave a very candid account of the role of, and impressions gathered by, the International Commission of Verification and Follow-up established under the Arias Peace Agreement. In this volume, since his remarks were off the record and since the commission's final report had been watered down under heavy pressure from the United States and the Central American governments most closely tied with Washington, we reproduce in this volume the previously leaked preliminary comments, observations, and conclusions of that commission in lieu of Vendrell's comments.

At the dinner banquet which followed, a unique perspective on the crisis as seen from state politics in the United States was presented. Carolyn Lukensmeyer, chief of staff of the office of Ohio Governor Richard Celeste, discussed the moral, legal, and political intricacies of the governor's decision to join other state governors in initially refusing to allow state National Guard units to participate in training exercises in Honduras near the Nicaraguan border. That evening Mexican Deputy Secretary of Foreign Affairs for International Cooperation Manuel Rodríguez Arriaga presented the keynote address. In it he outlined his country's position on the Contadora and subsequent peace processes, an ongoing saga in which he had personally been involved since 1983.

The events of the morning of 5 November featured an unusual head-to-head airing of opposing views by Robert Witajewski, country officer for Nicaragua at the U.S. Department of State, and Alejandro Bendaña, secretary-general of the Nicaraguan Ministry of Foreign Affairs. Their presentations were then commented upon by opposing think tank heads, L. Francis Bouchey, president of the Council on Inter-American Security (and coauthor of the famous *Santa Fe* Document of 1980), and William Goodfellow, director of the liberal Center for International Policy.

The conference concluded with a focus on the role of the U.S. media in the Central American drama. A presentation on "Covering Central America" by Fred Kiel, United Press International news director for Mexico and Central America, was followed by "A Critique of U.S. Media Coverage in Central America" by Jeff Cohen, founder and executive director of Fairness and Accuracy in Reporting.

Following the conference, each of the participants was provided with an audio tape of her/his presentation and asked to edit for style and minor errors and ambiguity. However, in order to document precisely and accurately the historical moment that the symposium represented, participants were urged not to update their presentations to include new events taking place subsequent to November 1988. In most cases, the participants stuck to those instructions. In the case where one did not, the individual himself alerts readers to that fact at the beginning of his contribution.

Bringing such a distinguished group of specialists and participants together and providing the type of infrastructural arrangements befitting such a gathering involved the expenditure of a considerable sum of money. Though the Department of Political Science at Ohio University was the principal coordinator and sponsor of the symposium, it received crucial financial support from additional entities at Ohio University. For this important assistance we thank the College of Arts and Sciences, the Center for International Studies, the Kennedy Lecture Series, the School of Journalism, the Baker Committee, the Contemporary History Institute, and the Student Activities Committee. Special thanks also go to departmental secretaries Dolly French and Linda Chapman as well as to a number of faculty members, students, and administrators who worked tirelessly to make the symposium a success.

We are also indebted to the Department of Political Science for its generous funding of aspects of the production of this volume including the typing of transcripts and expenditures faced by Sung Ho Kim in doing research in Washington, D.C. for his chapter. Finally, we wish to express our gratitude to William Goodfellow and the Center for International Policy in Washington for providing Professor Kim with access to its archives on the history of the peace process.

Thomas W. Walker

1

THE EMERGENCE OF THE PEACE PROCESS IN CENTRAL AMERICA

Sung Ho Kim

In November 1988, the peace process launched in January 1983 by Colombia, Mexico, Panama, and Venezuela (the four Contadora countries) and spurred on by the Esquipulas II accord of August 1987 was at a critical juncture with prospects for peace in Central America being uncertain. Prospects for peace were good because a temporary cease-fire between the Sandinista government of Nicaragua and the contra guerrillas reached at Sapoá (Nicaragua) the previous March was still holding. They were bad, however, because the talks leading to a permanent cease-fire which had begun in April were stalled. As observed by James Morrell in the February 1989 issue of *International Policy Report*, a pattern had developed in the talks in which each time agreement seemed near, the contras escalated their demands further "beyond what was required of Nicaragua by the Arias plan, until by June they were demanding a new constitution, forced resignation of the Supreme Court, and freedom for all draftees to leave the army immediately."[1]

It appeared as if the contras were trying to obtain at the conference table the capitulation of the Sandinista government which they could not achieve on the battlefield. Peace as an outcome of negotiations obviously was not what the contras had in mind, nor were the Sandinistas about to concede to the United States and give up their power in Nicaragua. Both parties were looking to Washington for direction, as the real drama of the Central American peace process was being played out as a contest between the Reagan administration and the U.S. Congress on the question of contra aid. Might one conjecture that

1

the Costa Rican peace plan was fading, as reported in the *Washington Post*?[2] According to a common theory of conflict resolution, however, third-party mediation is useful when both parties view the anticipated outcome of their negotiations to be preferable to the existing conflict. Moreover, third-party recommendations would be accepted more readily when the disputants want a peaceful resolution of their conflict but are unable to propose it first for fear of losing face or being perceived of as weak, thus having to settle for something less than otherwise might have been possible.

The main problem of Central American peace was the approach of the Reagan administration rather than the lack of mediation efforts. The prospects for peace through negotiations would remain dim as long as the Reagan administration maintained its policy of liberating Nicaragua from "Marxist" control and accepted the cost of pursuing the policy. Toward the end of the second term of the Reagan administration, however, such combined factors as the stalemate in the contra war, the Iran-Contra scandal in Washington, and general war-weariness in the region raised all hopes that both the Sandinista government and the United States might finally be willing to take their chances with the outcome of reasonably open and fair elections in Nicaragua. Acceptance of the idea of elections showed that the relentless peace process in Central America had indeed progressed in spite of earlier media pronouncements of its death. How did the Central American peace process all begin?

One could argue that the initial peace effort in Central America came from the Carter administration when it offered a successful revolutionary government in Nicaragua $118 million in aid in hopes of persuading the Sandinistas to sever their connection with the Farabundo Marti National Liberation Front (FMLN), the leftist guerrillas in El Salvador. Although the Carter administration had also spent $1 million in covert aid to internal oppositions in Nicaragua, the carrot was distinctly bigger than the stick in the Carter diplomacy. We cannot know whether the Carter policy of containing leftist revolution within the borders of Nicaragua would have succeeded. It would have been overly optimistic to expect a revolutionary government in Managua to have been tamed by an offer of economic aid. Nor could a full-blown insurgency in El Salvador have been controlled by stopping arms shipments through Nicaragua; the U.S. ambassador to Nicaragua, Lawrence Pezzullo, admitted such shipments to have been insignificant.[3]

In any case, when the United States terminated all aid to Nicaragua on 1 April 1981, despite Ambassador Pezzullo's report that the Sandinista government had halted transshipment of arms to guerrillas in El Salvador, it was clear that the Reagan administration was interested in something more than the containment policy pursued by the Carter administration.[4] A new policy became obvious with President Reagan's approval in November of a CIA proposal to use $19.95 million to organize a Latin American commando force of some five hundred men. The new policy had been authorized the previous March through his "Presidential Finding on Central America" submitted to Congress. The force was to "engage in paramilitary and political operations in Nicaragua," supplementing the one thousand anti-Sandinista Nicaraguans already in training in Honduras.[5]

It was in the context of these developments that the Reagan administration offered its version of peace to Nicaragua through the mission of Thomas Enders, then assistant secretary of state for Latin America. In a series of talks that began in Managua on 12 August between Enders and junta coordinator Daniel Ortega, the United States proposed its strict "neutrality" toward Nicaraguan exiles then in paramilitary training in the U.S., a bilateral nonaggression agreement, and resumption of economic aid to Nicaragua in return for an end to Nicaragua's alleged support for Salvadoran guerrillas and military buildup in Nicaragua. The Nicaraguan negotiators were angered by what they considered to be unreasonable demands from the United States. In October they rejected the U.S. offer as "sterile" because they were unsure whether the Enders proposal represented only the State Department's position without the blessing of the Reagan White House.[6]

The failure of the Enders talks strengthened the position of the hardliners in the Reagan administration. They were opposed to negotiations with the Sandinista government, preferring to have it overthrown. Thus, when the Reagan administration made its second peace offer in the form of an eight-point proposal presented to Nicaragua on 8 April 1982, the offer contained an important additional demand. Its point eight stipulated that "the first free elections" in Nicaragua be held as "essential elements of the political context of future relations between our two countries."[7] A week later, the Managua government responded with a thirteen-point proposal, expressing a "sincere disposition to begin serious negotiations." In August it proposed that Mexico participate in a meeting of foreign ministers with the United States to discuss the combined twenty-one

3

points. To this, the U.S. response took the form of a speech given by Enders on 20 August before the Commonwealth Club of San Francisco. By adding "democratic pluralism" in Nicaragua to the list of other demands, such as an end to support for foreign guerrilla movements and its arms buildup, as well as the removal of foreign military advisers, Enders was telling the Sandinistas not just to change its policies but themselves. Since the U.S. demand was made under an implied threat of a growing covert war against the Managua government, the Sandinistas were left with no choice but to fight on for their survival. The U.S. policy had shifted, and it appeared to many that the Reagan administration was increasing its demands as the Sandinistas were lowering theirs.[8]

European socialist groups were among the first to respond to the intensifying revolutionary violence in El Salvador and to the gathering cloud of war in Central America. As early as January 1981, the Socialist International tried its hand at mediation between the Salvadoran government and the FMLN, issuing its Communique on El Salvador in March 1981. This document called for a political settlement of the crisis in the region based upon the right of self-determination of the Salvadoran people and nonintervention from outside. In the same spirit, France issued a joint declaration with Mexico in August.

The most dynamic peace initiative, however, came from Mexico, which had an intense security interest in the region because of its shared common culture, geographical proximity, past experience of U.S. intervention, and fear of a spreading war. Because of Mexico's earlier objection to a U.S. effort to use an Organization of American States (OAS) peacekeeping force to prevent the Sandinistas from assuming power in Managua after General Somoza's fall from power in 1979, the Reagan administration was cool to the Mexican initiative. Thus, a comprehensive peace plan presented by the Mexican president José López Portillo in Managua on 21 February 1982, calling for an end to the training of Nicaraguan exiles by the United States and for a peace system based on nonaggression treaties between the United States and Nicaragua as well as between Nicaragua and its neighbors, went unheeded by the Reagan administration. Clearly, a time had come for a collective peace effort by a larger group of states in Latin America. These states might be able to formulate a peace plan which could put pressure on Nicaragua, the United States, and those Central American countries that were acting as U.S. proxies.

Thus the four foreign ministers of Colombia, Mexico, Panama, and Venezuela, meeting on 8-9 January 1983 on the small Panamanian island of Contadora, launched the peace process which had come to be known as the Contadora plan. After periodic meetings throughout the spring and summer months of 1983, the four Contadoran and five Central American governments managed to produce the Document of Objectives on 9 September. These meetings had included informal inquiries with some key U.S. officials and the occasional participation in the meetings by five Central American countries—Guatemala, Costa Rica, El Salvador, Honduras, and Nicaragua. The most significant perhaps of the twenty-one point document were strong statements about the objectives of democratization, national reconciliation, and verification. With respect to democratization, it called on all Central American countries

> to take measures leading to the establishment, or where appropriate, the improvement, of representative and pluralistic democratic systems that will guarantee the effective participation of the people in decision-making and ensure free access by the diverse tendencies of opinion to honest and periodic elections, based on the full observance of the rights of citizens.[9]

Following the pledge made in the Document of Objectives, the Contadoran negotiators continued to work toward the implementation of its objectives. The result was a much-amended draft of the "Contadora Act for Peace and Cooperation in Central America," presented to Central American governments on 7 September 1984 with the signing deadline set at 15 October.

The initial U.S. response to the draft Contadora treaty was positive. Calling it "an important step forward," Secretary of State George Shultz chided Nicaragua for rejecting "key elements of the draft, including those dealing with binding obligations to internal democratization and to reductions in arms and troop levels."[10] But when Nicaragua's President Daniel Ortega made a surprise move on 21 September to accept the act "in its totality [including the key elements referred to by Secretary Shultz], immediately and without modifications," the State Department suddenly found the treaty "unsatisfactory" and "one-sided," thus reversing its earlier endorsement.[11] What was one to make of this?

In some respects, the Contadora act was an extraordinary achievement toward peace in Central America. A product of what Roy Gutman calls "the most complex diplomatic effort of the modern era," involving at one point over one hundred technical experts and diplomats working in Panama City, the draft treaty provided for withdrawal of foreign military advisers, stopping all arms smuggling and imports as well as foreign military exercises, closing all foreign military bases, ending support for guerrilla movements, allowing free elections, and a commission of verification and control to investigate treaty violations.[12]

In accepting the September 1984 Contadora act, Nicaragua would have had to, in the words of William Goodfellow

1. Expel all Soviet bloc military advisers, estimated by the State Department to number between 2,500 and 3,500
2. Stop all imports of new Soviet weaponry, from Mi-24/Hind helicopters to AK-47 rifles
3. Shrink its 60,000-person army and scrap part of its inventory of weapons
4. End all types of aid to the Salvadoran guerrillas
5. Enter into a dialogue with the internal opposition
6. Let in a verification commission with powers of on-site inspection to verify all these commitments[13]

The draft Contadora treaty also called for the United States to stop its military exercises within thirty days and close down military bases and training centers in the region within six months. Fulfillment of these terms would have ended U.S. support for the contras.

Had the Reagan administration been willing to be satisfied with the achievement of only its declared purposes in Central America, that is, the denying of the Soviet bloc military presence in Central America, the draft Contadora treaty would have given the United States not only what it said it had wanted but also a way out of the contra war, which had become both troublesome in Congress and embarrassing in the society of sovereign states pledged to the principle of nonintervention.[14] As it turned out, the Contadora act was an unwelcome sideshow for the United States, which was bent on coercive diplomacy against Nicaragua.

The Contadora peace process, thus, was more successful in revealing the Reagan administration's real Central American policy goals of overthrowing the Sandinista government than in engaging the United States in a real peace process based upon a negotiated settlement. The

United States was not even a party to the Contadora negotiations. This was intentional on the part of the Contadora group, who wanted to produce a Central American peace accord with or without the blessing of the United States. They had hoped that if a peace accord could somehow be arranged for the Central American republics, a U.S. objection perhaps might be overcome or rendered irrelevant. Costa Rica, El Salvador, and Honduras, acting as U.S. proxies, however, did not play along with such a scheme, and soon made demands for further changes in the draft treaty. The result was a "counterdraft" offered by the foreign ministers of these three countries after meeting in Tegucigalpa, Honduras, on 19 October 1984. As expected, the U.S.-inspired counterdraft deleted restrictions on U.S. military exercises and bases in the region and even dropped the protocol which would have obligated the United States to observe the agreement.[15]

It was not until a year later that the Contadora countries could work out a compromise between the 7 September 1984 Contadora draft and the Tegucigalpa counterdraft. It was a year of intensifying conflict with political battles fought between containment and rollback strategists within the Reagan administration, between the Reagan White House and Congress over contra funding, and between the U.S.-supported paramilitary forces and Sandinistas in the field. It also was a year of escalating arms in the battle in which the Sandinista army introduced helicopter gunships. The outcome of the contra war, however, remained uncertain because of the on-and-off contra funding decisions by the U.S. Congress. Although the Second Boland Amendment in October 1984 suspended the use of funds by any government agencies for insurgency operations in Central America, the reelection in November of Ronald Reagan for his second term as president meant that the contra war was not over.

Meanwhile, in July 1985, the Contadora peace process had gained support from Argentina, Brazil, Peru, and Uruguay. These countries began consulting regularly with the original four Contadoran countries on the problems of Central American peace. An escalating conflict in the region along with the inability of the U.S.-supported contra rebels to establish themselves firmly as a viable insurgent force added to the sense of urgency that a diplomatic alternative be provided to an indecisive war.

Thus, by 12 September 1985, a modified draft Contadora treaty was ready for the Central American governments to review. In the first round of talks held on Contadora Island in early October, Costa Rica

7

expressed its willingness to sign the draft treaty. El Salvador and Honduras, however, had reservations, while Guatemala maintained its neutrality on the content of the draft treaty at least until after the upcoming elections. Nicaragua was not ready to declare its views then, but during the second round of negotiations later that month presented extensive objections to the modified draft. Nicaragua's position was to insist on a direct accommodation with the United States resulting in a nonaggression pact prior to any Contadora-sponsored agreement. A third round of negotiations was held among the Contadora plenipotentiaries in Panama in November, and some progress was achieved on verification and related issues; the prospects for peace through the Contadora, however, remained uncertain.

The spirit of Contadora returned with renewed energy when the eight foreign ministers of the Contadora group and the support group countries of Argentina, Brazil, Peru, and Uruguay, meeting in Caraballeda, Venezuela, on 11-12 January 1986 issued the "Caraballeda Message on Central America's Peace, Security and Democracy." Reiterating the 7 September 1984 Contadora draft which Nicaragua had already accepted, it called for simultaneous effort toward an end to contra aid and resumption of bilateral talks between the United States and Nicaragua. The Message was particularly significant in that it was issued in the wake of new presidential elections and a changing political climate in Central and Latin America toward democracy and neutrality in the U.S.-Nicaraguan dispute. The newly elected presidents, Vinicio Cerezo of Guatemala and Oscar Arias of Costa Rica, had already announced that they would remain neutral in the Nicaraguan conflict. The newly elected Honduran president, José Azcona Hoyo, campaigned on a platform that "the contra presence was unwanted and unconstitutional."[16]

The response to the Caraballeda Message thus was swift in Central America. Within three days, the foreign ministers of the five Central American states signed the Declaration of Guatemala, endorsing the latest Contadora statement. The following day, on 16 January, President Cerezo managed to extract additional endorsements from other Central American presidents who happened to be in Guatemala attending his inauguration.

Encouraged by the positive responses of the Central American governments to the Caraballeda Message, in early February the eight Contadora and support group foreign ministers took their conciliation effort to Washington. They failed in their attempt to see President

8

Reagan. However, they did hear Secretary of State Shultz propose talks between the U.S. and Nicaraguan governments on the one hand and the Unión Nicaraguense Opositor (United Nicaraguan Opposition, or UNO), an umbrella organization created by the Reagan administration to show a civilian face for the Nicaraguan contra forces, on the other. The Contadoran mediators returned home empty-handed.

Meanwhile the world's attention turned to a $100 million contra aid request which the Reagan administration made to Congress on 25 February. A huge effort at escalation of the contra operation, the sum requested from Congress—$70 million for arms and $30 million for nonlethal equipment—was nearly four times the $27 million approved the previous year and equal to the total amount expended during the preceding five years. Although the House of Representatives voted against the request on 23 March, its close 222-210 vote showed that a battle for war and peace in Central America was also being fought in the chambers of the U.S. Congress.

It was in the context of these developments that the Contadora and Central American negotiators met in Panama City on 5-6 April, hoping this time to give the finishing touch to a new draft treaty. They expected the meeting to be decisive for the Contadora peace process. In opening the meeting and speaking in the name of all the Contadora countries, Mexico proposed that the conference issue an appeal to the United States to suspend consideration of contra aid so as to allow time for Contadora negotiations to reach their conclusion. Costa Rica, Honduras, and El Salvador objected, while Nicaragua insisted on such an appeal. After three days of deadlocked conference, on 6 June twelve of the thirteen governments agreed to sign an agreement. Nicaragua refused. The Contadora effort failed again because Nicaragua, in the words of Goodfellow, "refused to agree to disarm in the face of the Reagan administration's military escalation."[17]

Before the signing deadline of 6 June, however, one last hope for agreement had remained. President Cerezo had arranged for the Central American presidents to meet at Esquipulas, Guatemala, on 24-25 May to iron out the differences that prevented the final agreement. This first Central American summit meeting since the Sandinista revolution, known as Esquipula I, however, ended in squabbles over the meaning of democracy with Nicaragua making the claim that it was already more democratic than some other Central American countries.

Meanwhile, in Washington a different kind of storm was blowing, this time over a letter to Representative Jim Slattery (D-Kan.)

9

from Philip Habib, who since March had been serving as special envoy for Central America. The letter, dated 11 April and bearing the signature of Habib, was in response to the inquiry made by liberal and centrist Democrats in Congress and was actually drafted at the State Department Bureau of Inter-American Affairs. It summed up the U.S. position on the Contadora peace initiative. The letter, which Habib claimed was cleared by Elliot Abrams and Oliver North, said that the United States understood the Contadora provisions to mean an end to contra aid "from the date of signature" of a verifiable Contadora agreement by all Central American governments.

The Habib letter appeared to offer a compromise between the Nicaraguan position of not signing until after the termination of contra aid and the U.S. position of not ending contra aid until after Nicaragua signed the Contadora agreement. The congressional right-wingers reacted to the Habib letter "with near panic," with Representative Jack Kemp (R.-N.Y.) demanding the dismissal of Ambassador Habib. They soon won their "struggle for the president's mind." On 23 May, the Reagan White House corrected itself by saying that the Habib letter should have promised an end to contra aid on implementation rather than on signature of the agreement.[18] The controversy over the Habib letter had an interesting effect on Nicaraguans, who, according to Gutman, wondered if the signing of the agreement would indeed put pressure on the United States to cut off contra aid as feared by the right-wingers in Washington.[19] On 27 May, President Daniel Ortega announced that he would sign the agreement on 6 June.

Thus, on 6 June when the Contadora mediators presented their third and final draft agreement for signature by the Central American countries, Nicaragua was prepared to sign it. At the same time the United States was distancing itself more completely than ever from what one official called a "lousy, fake, sham Contadora treaty."[20] The signing deadline of 6 June passed without signature and the Contadora peace process seemed to have come to the end of a road which had been marked by ups and downs since its inception in 1983. As if to mark the death of Contadora, on 25 June, the U.S. House of Representatives finally approved the $100 million contra aid request which it had rejected earlier. The Senate had approved it on 27 March. The Sandinista government responded with a crackdown on the opposition, closing down the newspaper *La Prensa* and strengthening its emergency laws. It would take something extraordinary to bring back life to a peace process in Central America.

Extraordinary events indeed did happen in the months leading to a new peace plan, the Central American Peace Accord, popularly known as Arias plan or Esquipulas II. The first of such extraordinary events was the embarrassing revelation in November, followed by a congressional investigation, of secret contra funding from the profits of weapon sales to Iran. This revelation undermined the Reagan administration's credibility. In the congressional elections of the same month, the Reagan administration also lost its Republican majority in the Senate.

The most important event of all, however, was the defection of Costa Rica from the U.S. proxy role. Having won the presidency on a peace platform, President Oscar Arias proceeded to rid the country of U.S. CIA agents, the CIA airstrip in northern Costa Rica, and hundreds of armed contras.[21] Arias then struck upon a novel idea of convening a meeting of the four Central American presidents, excluding Nicaragua, to arrange an agreement which then would be presented to Nicaragua "on a take-it-or-leave-it basis, and if Nicaragua refused, subject it to a form of boycott, obloquy, and isolation that would leave it wide open to American attack."[22]   Thus, on 15 February 1987, when the civilian presidents from El Salvador, Guatemala, and Honduras were invited to San José, Arias revealed his peace plan which included a cease fire, amnesty, dialogue between government and opposition, free elections, a halt in aid, and sanctuary to irregular forces. The four presidents agreed to invite Nicaragua to a five-nation summit to take place within ninety days.

The five-nation summit scheduled for 15 May, however, was postponed until August. By May, Costa Rica, Guatemala, and Nicaragua were in favor of the plan, but Honduras and El Salvador were not. At the Contadora-mediated meeting of the five Central American foreign ministers in Tegucigalpa in early August, Honduras argued successfully for inclusion in the revised peace plan of a cease-fire agreement between the Nicaraguan government and the guerrillas, something which the Nicaraguan government had been refusing to do. The original Arias plan only had mentioned the declaring of a cease-fire. Regarding aid to rebels, the Contadora mediators managed to change the word "suspending" to "cessation" and to include other types of aid besides military.[23]

A few days later, the five presidents of the Central American states converged on Guatemala City to mark a historical event in the four and one-half years of the Contadora and related negotiations. President Duarte's suggestion that a ninety-day deadline for compliance with treaty obligations would be more realistic than the original thirty-day deadline was quickly accepted by others. With Honduras' unwillingness to hold out for the United States as it had in the past fading, the eleven-point peace plan was ready. Two days later, on 7 August 1987, Oscar Arias Sanches of Costa Rica, José Napoleón Duarte of El Salvador, Vinicio Cerezo Arevalo of Guatemala, José Azcona Hoyo of Honduras, and Daniel Ortega Saavedra of Nicaragua finally placed their signatures on the Central American Peace Accord with detailed provisions for (1) national reconciliation, (2) cessation of hostilities, (3) democratization, (4) free elections, (5) cessation of aid to irregular forces and insurgent movements, (6) nonuse of territory to attack other states, (7) negotiations on security, verification, control, and limitation of weapons, (8) refugees and displaced persons, (9) cooperation, democracy, and freedom for peace and development, (10) international verification and follow-up, and (11) a timetable for implementing the commitments. There remained the real problems of implementation.

The Central American Peace Accord, popularly known as the Arias Plan, Esqipulas II, or Guatemala agreement, contained two important provisions for implementation. One was for an International Commission for Verification and Follow-up, composed of the two secretaries-general, or their representatives, of the Organization of American States and the United Nations, as well as the foreign ministers of Central America, the Contadora group, and the Support group. The other established a timetable for implementation. Ninety days were allowed "from the date of the signature" (that is, on or before 5 November) for "the commitments with regard to amnesty, cease-fire, democratization, cessation of aid to irregular forces or insurgent movements, and the non-use of territory to attack other states." These were to become operative "simultaneously and publicly." After 120 days from the date of signature (on or about 4 December), the International Commission for Verification and Follow-up (ICVF) was to analyze the progress made in the fulfillment of the agreements. Finally, after 150 days (on or after 3 January 1988) the five Central American presidents would meet to receive a report from the verification committee and "make pertinent decisions." However, as a result of the decisions made on 27-29 October by the Executive Commission, composed of the five Central American foreign ministers, the time limits for implementation were modified. Thus, the ICVF was requested to begin working immediately; the meeting of the Central American presidents was set "as of January

15th, 1988 in the city of San José, Republic of Costa Rica," rather than "after 150 days" from the signing of the treaty.[24]

The crucial first ninety days went rather well in Central America. The newspaper *La Prensa* and Radio Católica resumed operations in Nicaragua. The Sandinista government met with opposition parties in the national dialogue required in the peace agreement. Also, the governments of El Salvador and Guatemala met with the guerrillas in their country. There were two great surprises in this first period of implementation of the "Guatemala procedure." President Duarte, who was most reluctant to sign the Arias plan earlier, became its greatest proponent. On 5 November, the last day of the ninety-day deadline set for the implementation of treaty obligations, President Ortega went beyond the terms of the Arias agreement. He announced indirect negotiations with the contras to work out a cease-fire, thus ending the no-talk-with-contra position stubbornly held by the Sandinista government since 1981.[25]

Thus, by 14 January 1988, when the 118-page ICVF report was submitted to Central American presidents for review, internal political dialogues with unarmed opposition parties had been established in all five Central American countries. Amnesty decrees had been issued in all applicable countries. An El Salvador amnesty was "misapplied." The freeing of all five hundred prisoners included "death-squad" killers and contributed to the "climate of impunity" in that country. National Reconciliation Commissions similarly were established in all five countries. Varying degrees of press and other freedoms had also been reported in Central American countries inching toward democracy. The major stumbling block to the Guatemala peace process, however, remained: the continuing American aid to the contras.[26]

Washington had, of course, changed. The godfathers of the contra war, William Casey and Oliver North, were no longer in office. With its credibility seriously undermined by the Iran-Contra scandal, the Reagan administration was more vulnerable to outside pressure than before. The growing international support for the Arias peace plan—the Nobel Peace Prize was awarded to Arias on 13 October—and the personal pleas by Presidents Duarte and Azcona to give peace a chance managed to persuade the Reagan administration to postpone its threatened request for some $270 million in contra aid until after 1988.[27] The aid to the contras finally came to an end on 3 February 1988 when the House of Representatives voted down by a margin of eight votes

(219-211) the administration's request for $36.25 million in mixed lethal and nonlethal aid to the contras.

The congressional rejection of the contra aid request in February was an important signal that the Arias peace procedure would be given a chance. The cutoff of U.S. aid was intended to force the contras to move from the battlefield to the conference table while the narrow margin in the congressional vote warned the Sandinistas that the contra funding could be revived. Thus, in mid-March, direct cease-fire talks between the Sandinista government and the contras without a mediator replaced earlier indirect talks with Cardinal Miguel Obando y Bravo, the leading Roman Catholic prelate in Nicaragua and an influential churchman opposed to the Sandinistas, as a mediator. The earlier talks had been stalled because of intensified contra attacks on northern towns in December 1987. These had been followed by the Nicaraguan army's hot pursuit into Honduras in February and March 1988, triggering a three thousand–troop deployment by the United States to counter the Nicaraguan "invasion."[28] The appointment of Defense Minister Humberto Ortega as head of the government delegation, and the proposal to hold talks on Nicaraguan soil without mediator, signaled the seriousness of the new talks.

The cease-fire agreement signed by the Nicaraguan government and contras at Sapoá on 23 March was arguably the greatest achievement of the Arias peace plan in that it was the "first true agreement between warring factions." The contra war, however, was not yet over; the Sapoá agreement only suspended it. Some fierce fighting had been fought during the cease-fire talks. The contras were still entitled to humanitarian aid and weapons while a permanent cease-fire was being negotiated for the terms of their relocation and eventual participation in the national dialogue and political parties. There would be hard days ahead. As previously mentioned, the permanent cease-fire talks had developed a pattern of escalating demands by the contras.

To make the Sapoá agreement possible, the Sandinista government made two important concessions beyond the requirements of the Arias plan: (1) it included the contras in the national dialogue before they had laid down their arms and accepted amnesty, and (2) it would discuss the question of military draft. Following the contra rejection of a comprehensive proposal for a permanent cease fire which it had built on the Arias plan and offered to the contras on 17 April, the government again agreed to a list of political reforms suggested by Alfredo Cesar, who initiated behind-the-scenes talks with government negotiators,

14

American lawyer Paul Reichler and Humberto Ortega. Some of the reforms to which the government formally agreed during the 26-28 May talks in Managua were once again beyond the requirement of the Arias plan: (1) the separation of state powers, (2) the equalization of the privileges of all political parties by detaching the army and police from the ruling party and reducing the power of the Sandinista mass organizations, and (3) the transfer of power to set certain election dates from the constitutionally-mandated electoral council to the national dialogue with contra participation.[29]

The hoped-for agreement, however, did not materialize. The contra faction, headed by former Somozist National Guard colonel Enrique Bermúdez, proposed additional demands which called for a new constitution and suspension of the military draft. When the contras returned to the final round of talks on 7-9 June, they added yet more demands which included the right of draftees to leave the army at will; forced resignation of the supreme court justices to be replaced by professionals chosen from "slates of three for each position proposed by the government party, the opposition parties, and the Nicaraguan resistance"; and the restoration of seized contra property that had been distributed to smallholders or cooperatives. Imagine the Sandinista government having to "carry out these actions, some of them unconstitutional, while the contra army remained armed and in its enclaves; the contras would take until 31 January 1989 to disarm, i.e., until they had a chance to see who won the U.S. presidential elections." These were the types of demands that, as noted by the CIP's "International Policy Update" of 13 June 1988, would indeed have come from a "victorious army or were measures that a victorious political party might enact upon taking over the government." Since the Sandinistas had not been defeated militarily in the field or politically at home, were these demands designed to "torpedo the negotiations and throw the issue back once more to a divided U.S. Congress"?[30]

Not surprisingly, in July the U.S. Congress again became occupied with the contra aid issue when Senator Robert Dole proposed $27 million in nonmilitary aid with a provision for a second vote in September for $20 million in new military aid. Although Democratic senators were united in backing a measure proposed on 5 August by majority leader Senator Robert Byrd to keep the delivery of nonmilitary aid out of the hands of the CIA, in conformity with the Sapoá agreement, and delaying the congressional voting on lethal contra aid, the prospect for contra aid in the future was far from dead. The central

15

question became one of determining the appropriate U.S. foreign policy, particularly with respect to its contra war.

The United States was a hegemonic power in Central America. It did not have the "right" to intervene in the internal and external affairs of Central America, but it undeniably had the "privilege" of power to do so. The academic debate in the United States over contra aid, therefore, was largely one of weighing claims based on "right" as articulated in the terms of moral and legal discourses, against those based on the "privilege" of power in the context of *Realpolitik*.

Confusing to the general public, however, was that the claims based on "privilege" were always presented in the rhetorical language of moral discourse so that they might win popular support. Public debate, as distinct from an academic seminar, did not discuss dispassionately the relative merits of moral principles against the constraint of political realism in seeking balanced considerations for peace and justice in Central America. Because the wider public understands the familiar language of morality better than academic discourses on political realism, governments frequently resort to disinformation campaigns, while the opposition and critics typically confront it with a truthful or counterdisinformation campaign.

The standard defense of U.S. policy, accordingly, had been to blame outside intervention for the problems of peace in Central America. "Whatever the social and economic conditions that invited insurgency in the region," contended President Reagan's National Bipartisan Commission on Central America (the Kissinger Commission) in its 1984 report, "outside intervention is what gives the conflict its present character." The report listed as all important in both morale and operational terms propaganda support, money, sanctuary, arms supplies, training, communications, intelligence, logistics. "Without such support from Cuba, Nicaragua, and the Soviet Union," concluded the report, "neither in El Salvador nor elsewhere in Central America would such an insurgency pose so severe a threat to the government."[31] The only appropriate policy choice left for the United States, therefore, was to contain the Marxist revolution within the borders of Nicaragua or to roll it back to before the times of Ortega or even Castro.

To the critics of U.S. Central American policy, the principal obstacle to peace in the region thus was the rollback policy of the Reagan administration, which had been unwilling to accept any modification in the external and internal policies of the Sandinista government. It was not that the Reagan administration was a monolith. In an incisive analysis of U.S. policy in Nicaragua from 1981 to 1987,

Gutman provides us with a detailed account of the policy disputes within the Reagan administration between those who saw no realistic alternative to containment in Central America, and those who wanted rollback to the status quo ante-Sandinistas.[32] The President's role, of course, was decisive in adopting the rollback policy, with CIA Director William Casey as its principal architect. The critics charged that President Reagan himself was an ideologue whose view of the government in Managua was not based on reality but on the essentialist preconception of the Marxist revolutionaries; therefore he was incapable of finding a compromise solution to the problems of revolutionary violence in the region.

What emerged from these considerations, then, were the four basic issues of peace in Central America: the original revolutionary violence, the alleged outside support, the claim of defensive counter-intervention by the United States, and the specific rollback policy of the Reagan administration. The rhetoric of the Reagan administration and the congressional critics was largely an effort to influence public perception and judgment on these issues.

There is little doubt that the initial issue of peace in Central America was revolutionary violence, which was generally understood to have arisen from the social and economic conditions of the region. Even the Kissinger Commission had admitted the domestic origins of insurgency in Central America. What, then, explained the Central American rebellions? How justifiable were they in terms of human rights, social justice, and national self-determination?

Of the causal explanations of Central American rebellions, probably the most sophisticated is the rapid impoverishment of agrarian and urban workers who have become victimized by the so-called externally oriented dependency growth of Central American economies under the control of socially irresponsible elites. Thus, according to John A. Booth and Thomas W. Walker, what "has led to political turmoil and rebellion in three of the region's countries since 1971" was not the "long-term, grinding deprivation" of Central Americans but the "relative deprivation of becoming rapidly poorer—declining living standards among large segments of the population."[33]

If rebellions were an understandable and even a justifiable action by the dispossessed and impoverished in a condition of gross and worsening economic inequity and social injustice in certain parts of Central America, what was the role of outside support in the Central American rebellions? Was it, as the Kissinger report charged, "what gives the conflict its present character," thus warranting appropriate

17

U.S. counterintervention? This, of course, had been the central issue in the public debate over contra aid.

There is little doubt that spontaneous rebellions require leadership and organization to develop into a sustained revolutionary movement aimed at seizing power. To what extent, then, was the outside support responsible for the transformation of ordinary rebellions into a sustained revolutionary movement in Nicaragua and El Salvador? This was an important issue because U.S. hegemony in Central America would be justifiable to the extent that it was perceived as playing a protective role in defense of the common interest of the hemispheric nations.

Thus, an old U.S. claim that communism is an ideological threat which warrants defensive collective intervention against its establishment in the Western Hemisphere received the most forceful expression during the Reagan administration.[34] Such a claim became particularly important for the Reagan administration, which was determined to pursue an anti-Sandinista campaign even after the alleged outside support in arms and logistics either had ceased to be or had become no longer an overwhelming issue.[35]

Because the very existence of Marxist governments in Central America became the central issue in the contra war debate in the United States, the Reagan administration had to confront congressional critics, who were as scornful of the irresponsible elites in Central America as they were of revolutionary violence. The administration also had to overcome a hollowness, especially in the historical context of growing Latin American nationalism, in the proposition that communism was more evil than U.S. interventionism. With the Iran-Contra scandal exploding in the face of the Reagan administration at the end of 1986, its rollback policy finally appeared to have come to an end. But it did not. After all, a very popular president of the mightiest nation on earth was at the helm of a secret war waged against a tiny country with a government of suspect ideology. The Reagan administration was indeed capable of prolonging indefinitely the misery of destruction and war on Nicaragua as the people of Nicaragua, who might originally have welcomed the Sandinista revolution, were showing signs of war-weariness and were eager to settle for peace rather than a romantic vision of the revolutionary Nicaragua.

The complex problems of Central American peace could thus be reduced to the Reagan administration's hostility toward the Sandinista government in Nicaragua and its unwillingness to take a chance with a process of negotiations, which might have resulted in the Sandinista government remaining in power in Managua. What would finally persuade the Reagan administration, or its successor, to take that chance?

NOTES

1. James Morrell, "The Nine Lives of the Central American Peace Process," *International Policy Report* (February 1989): 7.

2. Morrell, "The Nine Lives," 7.

3. William Goodfellow, "The Diplomatic Front," in *Reagan Versus the Sandinistas: The Undeclared War on Nicaragua*, ed. Thomas W. Walker (Boulder, Colorado: Westview Press, 1987), 144.

4. For an excellent analysis of what Roy Gutman believes to be the Reagan administration's first major mistake in cutting off aid to Nicaragua, see his *Banana Diplomacy: The Making of American Policy in Nicaragua 1981-1987* (New York: Simon & Schuster, 1988), 35-38.

5. Peter Kornbluh, "The Covert War," in *Reagan Versus the Sandinistas*, ed. Thomas W. Walker, 21-38.

6. For an insightful analysis of a proud revolutionary government in Managua failing to see the necessity to "go more than half way, much more than half way, to satisfy the Americans," see Goodfellow, "Diplomatic Front," 144-46.

7. Gutman, *Banana Diplomacy*, 95.

8. Gutman, *Banana Diplomacy*, 88-120.

9. Gutman, *Banana Diplomacy*, 166.

10. Goodfellow, "Diplomatic Front," 149.

11. Goodfellow, "Diplomatic Front," 149.

12. Gutman, *Banana Diplomacy*, 225.

13. Goodfellow, "Diplomatic Front," 150.

14. For an analysis of the development of the principle of nonintervention as a binding obligation among the American states, see Sung Ho Kim, "The Issues of International Law, Morality, and Prudence," in *Reagan Versus the Sandinistas*, ed. Thomas W. Walker, 266-73.

15. Goodfellow, "Diplomatic Front," 151.

16. Gutman, *Banana Diplomacy*, 327. Azcona reversed his position later as a result of pressure from the United States and his own military.

17. Goodfellow, "Diplomatic Front," 152.

18. Goodfellow, "Diplomatic Front," 153.

19. Gutman, *Banana Diplomacy*, 330; Goodfellow, "Diplomatic Front," 154.

20. Goodfellow, "Diplomatic Front," 154.

21. Morrell, "Nine Lives," 3.

22. Morrell, "Nine Lives," 3.

23. Morrell, "Nine Lives," 4.

24. FLACSO (Latin American Faculty of Social Sciences), UPEACE (University for Peace, created by U.N. Res. 35/55/5/XII/1980), and CSUCA (Central American Superior Council of Universities), *Second White Paper on Advances Achieved in the Process of Fulfilling the Peace Accord for Central America "Esquipulas II" Second Period: Nov. 6, '87-Jan. 16, '88* (San Jose: FLASCO, 1988), 9.

25. Morrell, "Nine Lives," 5.

26. Thus, at the ICVF meeting in Panama on 13 January, the five Central American governments agreed to include in the summary report of the commission a statement which explicitly called on the United States to cease contra aid as "an indispensable requirement for the success of the peace efforts and of this Procedure as a whole," Center for International Policy,

"Central Americans Call on U.S. to End Aid to Contras," *International Policyy Update* (January 14, 1988), 1.

27. Gutman, *Banana Diplomacy*, 354.

28. Gutman, *Banana Diplomacy*, 6.

29. Center for International Policy, "The Nicaraguan Cease-Fire Talks: A Documentary Survey," *International Policy Update* (June 13, 1988).

30. Center for International Policy, "Nicaraguan Cease-Fire."

31. Cited in John A. Booth and Thomas W. Walker, *Understanding Central America* (Boulder, Colorado: Westview Press, 1989), 47.

32. Gutman, *Banana Diplomacy*.

33. Booth and Walker, *Understanding Central America,* 14.

34. As exemplified most clearly in the "Declaration of Solidarity for the Preservation of the Political Integrity of American States Against the Intervention of International Communism," adopted at the Tenth Inter-American Conference at Caracas in 1954; see D. A. Graber, *Crisis Diplomacy: A History of U.S. Intervention Policies and Practices* (Washington, D.C.: Public Affairs Press, 1959), 308.

35. The most articulate exponent of the claim of justifiable counterintervention in defense of prior "ideological" intervention is John Norton Moore. See his *The Secret War in Central America: Sandinista Assault on World Order* (Frederick, Maryland: University Publications of America, Inc., 1987); "The Secret War in Central America and the Future of World Order," *American Journal of International Law* 80/43 (1986).

2

THE UNITED STATES AND LATIN AMERICA: HISTORIC CONTINUITIES, NEW DIRECTIONS

Howard J. Wiarda

Latin America, especially Central America and the Caribbean, recently has been catapulted onto our television screens and the front pages of our newspapers—if not yet into our consciousness.* A major debate has been occurring in the United States about what our policy toward Latin America should be. This debate often has been intensely partisan and ideological. It has not always been enlightening.

If one probes beneath the partisan posturing, the emotionalism of the debate, and the veil of untruths and half-truths surrounding this issue, one discovers that there are critical aspects of past and present U.S. policy towards Latin America that have not received sufficient attention. The first of these is the historic continuity of American foreign policy in Latin America, including its practice by the most recent two American administrations, those of Presidents Carter and Reagan. The second is the learning and growth process which, again, all recent American administrations have gone through with regard to Latin America policy. The third is the remarkable degree of consensus, often hidden under the avalanche of partisan differences, that exists on most aspects of U.S. Latin America policy. And the fourth is, in the wake of Irangate and a weakened presidency, how fragile and uncertain the possibilities for an enlightened U.S. policy toward Latin America still are.

---

*An earlier version of this paper was presented as the 3rd Annual Ellsworth Lecture, Johnson State College, Johnson, Vermont, and published by the college.

The Context of U.S.-Latin American Relations

Let us begin by talking about the context of U.S.-Latin American relations and by stating some truths that may not leave us entirely comfortable.

1. Latin America historically has not been thought of as a very important area in the rank ordering of U.S. policy priorities. Washington views the Soviet Union, Europe and NATO, China, Japan, and the Middle East as more important than Latin America. Latin America's low priority is changing under the impact of the crisis in Central America and as Hispanics have become a major influence in our domestic politics. But the rate of these changes seems glacial. Latin America still has a low priority and policy makers do not pay the area much sustained or serious attention.

2. The United States does not understand Latin America very well. We tend to view the region through the prism of our own preferred solutions. We do not seriously study its culture, history, politics, and sociology. Instead we think that we know best for the area, that our ways are the ways Latin America should adopt. We are certain either that Central America is "another Vietnam" or, alternatively, that we are finally overcoming our "Vietnam complexes" there. In neither case do we try to understand the Central American crisis in its own terms. As an illustration, when I worked for Dr. Henry Kissinger as lead consultant to the National Bipartisan Commission on Central America, I wrote a report for the commissioners suggesting that we attempt some unaccustomed deference toward the region, that we try to understand Central American institutions in their own right, that we consider allowing the Central Americans to work out their own murky solutions to their own murky problems. That suggestion received no support from the commissioners on either side of the political aisle. The sense is very strong in this country, among both liberals and conservatives, that we know best for Central America and must impose our solutions on it.

3. Not only do we not understand Latin America very well, but we do not want to understand it. That attitude is best summed up in the oft-quoted comment of *New York Times* correspondent James Reston: "The United States will do anything for Latin America except read about it." Not only do we not read about the area, but

we consistently use the wrong models to try to understand and reform it. The course of U.S.-Latin American relations is a path strewn with cast-off theories that in Latin America have not worked very well or as intended: Rostow's aeronautical "stages of growth," the Alliance for Progress, the political development ideas of the 1960s, and a host of others. None of these have worked because they have not been adapted adequately to Latin American realities.

These factors, based either on ignorance or on some set of academic or ideological blinders, prevent us from understanding Latin America on its own terms and in its own institutional context. When such blinders are worn by policy makers as well as academics, it is small wonder that our policies toward the region often have been misinformed and misapplied. The fact is that at the base of our policy mistakes toward Latin America is a whole range of cultural, social, and political attitudes and prejudices toward that region that are strongly rooted in myths, half-truths, and misunderstandings.

Historic Continuities of Policy

Within this context of what may be termed traditional bias, misunderstanding, and ethnocentrism, let us look at the historic bases and continuities of U.S. policy toward Latin America. The fundamentals have remained the same for a long time. They have not changed greatly since President Monroe in his famous doctrine first articulated them 167 years ago. A more modern and updated version, formulated at the time a century ago when the United States emerged as a major global power, was set forth by Teddy (later President) Roosevelt and Admiral Alfred Thayer Mahan, the apostle of American seapower. The "bedrocks" of U.S. policy then (and largely now) included the following:

1. Keep out hostile foreign powers. In earlier eras that meant efforts directed against Spain, France, England, and Germany; more recently it has meant excluding the Soviet Union from the region as much as possible.
2. Maintain stability. Latin America has not been known for its stable politics. Indeed the very instability of the area has given foreign powers the opportunity to establish beachheads there. Hence, the

United States has been very concerned in the region to secure stability. Maintaining stability means not some unalterable defense of the status quo but encompasses adjustment to and even the encouragement of change and modernization. But not change that gets out of hand or leads to revolution.
3. Maintain a string of bases, listening posts, and stations throughout Central America and the arc of the Caribbean islands.
4. Maintain access to markets, raw materials, and labor supplies of the area; keep open the sea lanes; guard the Panama Canal and the routes to it; provide border protection; stand for free trade and navigation.

There are some corollaries that follow from this listing of our primary interests in Latin America. First, as a nation historically we have been far more concerned with the areas close to home, on our strategic southern flank, Central America and the Caribbean, than with South America. Second, given the nature of these bedrock interests and of U.S. indifference to Latin America generally, our policy has almost always been reactive and crisis-oriented rather than anticipatory. We have tended to react to crises after they occur—Guatemala in 1954, Cuba in 1959-1961, the Dominican Republic in 1965, Chile in 1973, Central America today—rather than develop a long-term and positive program for the region. The third corollary has to do with democracy and human rights. These aspects generally have been subordinated to the strategic fundamentals listed above; where there has been a conflict between them, strategic considerations have dominated. But presently that is changing; human rights now are being viewed as ways to achieve stability in Latin America, as the best barriers against communism, and as the best means to undercut the appeals of a hostile foreign power.

Over the last hundred years and more, there has been very little disagreement from administration to administration, whether Democrat or Republican, on these basic goals of American foreign policy. The strategic considerations have been remarkably consistent. The only question has been the relative emphasis to be given each of these strategic fundamentals and the most effective and appropriate means to achieve those ends.

The question relates to a familiar one in American foreign policy, the debate between realism and idealism. Realists have generally believed that U.S. foreign policy is best served by assistance to dictators or military regimes that are visibly, publicly, and sometimes brutally anticommunist. Such dictators, they argue, provide stability, take vigorous action against communism, and are generally amenable to U.S. interests. Idealists believe that U.S. interests are best served by being on the side of democracy and human rights, by abandoning the dictators and oligarchs, and by siding with Latin America's so-called "new forces." The idealists, in accord with the moralistic and missionary tradition that has long characterized American foreign policy, believe that it is the obligation of the United States not just to adjust to changing conditions in Latin America but to lead and push for change—sometimes regardless of the wishes of Latin America.

American administrations—and American foreign policy—have often oscillated between these two poles. At one time we have appeared tough and hard-nosed, at others soft and idealistic. But most recent American administrations have sought to balance and reconcile these conflicting tendencies. We have sought to protect U.S. strategic interests and advance democracy and human rights at one and the same time. Moreover, in recent years we have tended to see the two not as in conflict but complementary. Democracy, development, and human rights may be viewed as part of a single and coordinated policy aimed at securing stability and modernization, and keeping out hostile foreign powers. It is the dictators—Batista or Somoza—and strong-arm regimes that have proven to be unstable; further, rather than serving as bastions of anticommunism, such regimes may provide the conditions in which communism and radicalism may flourish. That was of course the great lesson of the Cuban revolution.

Recall, however, that the goals of U.S. foreign policy largely have been set: stability, anticommunism, bases, sea lanes, no hostile foreign powers. These are the givens in any administration. The main questions in our foreign policy debate, including the present debate over Central America, are the best means to achieve these goals, not the goals per se.

Therefore, generally there has been far more continuity in U.S. policy toward Latin America than has been thought. In fact, our policy has been remarkably continuous over the last century because the goals are given. We still disagree over the best or most efficient strategies to achieve these goals but rarely over the goals themselves. In fact, the continuities, from Eisenhower to Kennedy, from Kennedy to Johnson, from Johnson to Nixon-Ford, and from Ford to Carter have been remarkable. The faces change, there is always some nuance in each new administration, some new emphasis as we try to grapple with this part of the world which we neither admire nor to which we pay much serious attention, but the essentials of policy have remained quite consistent over all this time.

These notions of continuity apply, despite the hot campaign rhetoric and the sometimes fierce contemporary debate, even to the transition from Carter to Reagan—two presidents whom we often think of as polar opposites in their approach to foreign policy. Carter began his administration with a foreign policy in considerable part derived from the left wing of the Democratic Party. Reagan began from a base in the right wing of the Republican Party. Both of these recent presidents gravitated over time back toward the center, back toward the mainstream of American foreign policy. With particular regard to the transition from Carter to Reagan, let me now examine how that process worked, what its dynamics were, and what it meant for future U.S. policy.

The Transition from Carter to Reagan

In 1980-1981, it appeared as though there would be a sharp break in American foreign policy. Candidate Reagan and his aides were strongly critical of the Carter approach. They faulted Carter for his romantic and globalist approach to the Third World; for emphasizing human rights at the expense of more fundamental U.S. security interests; for "losing" Grenada and Nicaragua; for alienating such key countries as Argentina, Brazil, and Chile; and for allowing the real possibility to develop of other guerrilla triumphs in El Salvador and Guatemala.

In the campaign statements of Reagan and in the transition documents prepared by his foreign policy team, it appeared as though there would now be less attention to human rights, more stress on East-West (as opposed to North-South) issues, less attention to public foreign assistance and more to private investment, greater realism and less idealism in foreign policy, more focus on the Soviet Union, strenuous effects to roll back the guerilla challenge in Latin America, and efforts to reach accommodations with authoritarian regimes which could then be reformed rather than treated as enemies.

The differences in the Carter and Reagan approaches, at least as they were presented during the campaign and in position papers prepared by President-elect Reagan's foreign policy advisers, seemed clear and rather stark. They were so stark that in 1984 and 1988, the Democrats fought the 1980 election all over again. Many politically activist

Americans also came to believe that the campaign rhetoric that prevailed in 1980 was still the basis of Reagan administration foreign policy eight years later. But that view ignores the enormous evolution in administration policy that occurred after 1980, the learning process that took place, and the domestic and bureaucratic pressures that forced Reagan administration policy back toward the center, toward the mainstream of American foreign policy. Precisely the same gravitation toward the middle—albeit beginning from the opposite side of the political spectrum—had occurred under President Carter. By ignoring these dynamics we miss a great deal in our understanding of Reagan administration foreign policy, and in our understanding of the Bush administration.

We cannot here review all the shifts in Reagan administration policy, but let us briefly examine the record on the major issues, both to get a sense of the shifts that occurred within the administration and to emphasize how continuous and consistent the policy was with the classic tradition of policy as outlined earlier. For example, in the human rights area a very strong case can be made that after a terribly shaky and sometimes unfortunate beginning, the human rights record of the Reagan administration, in terms of actual accomplishments as distinct from rhetoric, was at least as strong as that of the Carter administration. In addition, the two main positive foreign policy initiatives of the Reagan administration, the Caribbean Basin Initiative and the Kissinger Commission recommendations on Central America, both bear a striking resemblance to the Alliance for Progress of John F. Kennedy—particularly in the balances they strike between socioeconomic assistance and military aid, public assistance and private investment. A strong case can be made that the Reagan administration did more—or at least as much—to advance the cause of democracy in Latin America than did its predecessor. Ninety percent of the people of Latin America, thanks in part to U.S. pressures, now live under democratic rule—the highest percentage in the history of the hemisphere.

If one turns to policy toward individual countries, the same conclusions largely apply: that there was far more continuity than change in U.S. policy, and that the policy itself was far more pragmatic, centrist, and moderate than the ongoing political debate suggests. For example, U.S.-Cuban relations remain in a deep freeze, but it was actually during the Carter administration that the strong disillusionment began with the policy of gradually normalizing relations with the Cuban regime. In El Salvador both the Carter and the Reagan administrations

28

pursued a policy designed to encourage the formation of a democratic-centrist government, to isolate and reform the far right, and to isolate and, if possible, defeat the guerrilla left. Policy toward Nicaragua has been the most controversial, but both the Carter and the Reagan administrations agreed on (1) the growing Marxism-Leninism of the Sandinista regime; (2) its steadily closer ties with the Soviet Union; (3) the increasingly monolithic and nonpluralist nature of the regime; (4) the need to isolate the revolution and keep it from spreading; (5) the need to put pressure on the regime (although there may still be disagreement on the precise form such pressure should take) while at the same time keeping open the possibilities for negotiation and compromise.

In all these and other cases, U.S. policy was consistently more pragmatic, more centrist, and more middle-of-the-road than the early campaign rhetoric would have led one to believe. Indeed the parallels between the later-Carter and later-Reagan policies are striking—much to the chagrin, incidentally, of the ideological true believers in both the Carter and the Reagan camps. Hence we need to ask, What are the factors explaining these remarkable parallels and continuities in U.S.-Latin American policy?

Answers may be provided by examining both domestic and international factors. Domestically, the press has played a major role. Concerned about its reelection possibilities, wanting a good press, and responding to the drumbeat of criticism it received on El Salvador and other issues, the Reagan administration was sensitive to the press and modified its policies accordingly. The Congress was another factor, forcing compromise by holding hearings on administration policy, requiring certification of human rights progress in difficult countries like El Salvador and Guatemala, holding up presidential appointments, and seeking to frustrate and embarrass the Republican White House as much as possible.

Such new domestic interests as the human rights lobbies and religious groups also forced a sometimes reluctant administration back toward the center. Public opinion, which favored no more "second Cubas" in the Caribbean but was reluctant to give the government the instruments to carry out that mandate (no foreign aid, no CIA covert operations, no commitment of U.S. ground forces) also played a major role.

In addition, bureaucratic factors were important. The Defense Department was reluctant to get involved in another Vietnam in Central

America. There were changes in the Department of State, personified by the emergence and consolidation of foreign policy decision making under George Shultz, that led toward centrism. Meanwhile, about two years into the administration (about the same time period as under Carter), the professionals and specialists within the several foreign policy bureaucracies reconsolidated their grip on policy, slowly recapturing policy making from the more ideological appointees who had accompanied President Reagan into office. While these changes were occurring, the administration was itself going through a learning process about Central America and key foreign policy issues.

On the international front other forces were working that similarly led to greater centrism of policy. The civil war in El Salvador proved not to be subject to a simplistic East-West interpretation (Soviet machinations) but required a North-South (poverty, social conditions) explanation as well. In addition, the administration discovered that the levers of power in El Salvador were not as easily manipulable as it had thought. Even in small countries such as this, it proved far more difficult than the administration had expected to grasp these levers and effect change. The handles of Salvadoran society and politics proved to be very slippery or they broke off in the administration's hands as it attempted to aid, assist, and rearrange them.

Finally, that amorphous factor called world public opinion played an important role in changing administration policies. The Reagan administration found that a number of our friends, allies, and neutrals did not support U.S. policy in Central America. Hence, the administration began to push for democracy, human rights, and socioeconomic progress in the region as well as U.S. strategic interests, narrowly defined. Friends and allies, to say nothing of the Congress and U.S. domestic public opinion and interest groups, could be neutralized, silenced, and in some cases even brought around to supporting U.S. policy if it stood for democracy, human rights, and development, and not just for its security aspects. Not only could domestic and international opponents of U.S. policy be neutralized, but the administration discovered that democratic and centrist regimes in Latin America were far less bellicose, far easier to get along with, and caused far fewer problems for the U.S. than authoritarian regimes of the right or left. Hence, the administration again shifted course in favor of a policy that supported a trend already under way in Latin America, away from authoritarianism and toward democracy. For reasons moral, political, and *Realpolitik*, the administration came to a position of strong support for democracy and democratic transitions in Latin America and launched the Democracy Project and National Endowment for Democracy to help strengthen its policies.

The Evolution of Administration Policy

Some of the early statements of Reagan administration officials on Latin America were strident and unfortunate. On the other hand, the Democratic opposition continued to respond as if these early statements were still administration policy.

Actually, there was a significant evolution from the more ideological language of the early weeks of the administration. We did not "go to the source" (as Secretary of State Haig once suggested, with obvious references to Cuba); we did not invade Nicaragua; we did not send U.S. combat forces to fight in Central America.

On the positive side, the administration achieved a major (though still uncertain) victory in El Salvador, it maintained a strong human rights program, and through Project Democracy and the National Endowment for Democracy it came out four-square and strongly assisted the evolution toward democracy throughout the hemisphere. Through the Caribbean Basin Initiative and the Kissinger Commission legislative agenda it developed a balanced program of aid and investment, socioeconomic and military assistance, moral (human rights, democracy) as well as strategic concerns.

More than that, the administration had begun to put our relations with Latin America on the same normal, healthy, mature, regular, almost boring basis that we have long held with Western Europe. This is not to say there are no issues of contention between the United States and the countries of Latin America; there are, and they are many. These differences will continue to exist regardless of the governments in power in Washington or in Latin America because on a variety of issues we have somewhat different interests. But such issues are now handled largely through diplomatic and normal bilateral channels rather than on the crash or crisis basis of the past. Given the past history of U.S. relations with Latin America, of crisis response and frequent interventions, such boring and normal relations seem to me to have represented a step in the right direction.

Even on Nicaragua—our most contentious issue—there was widespread agreement in Washington, D.C., if not yet on college campuses and among church or Hollywood groups. Almost no one disagreed anymore that Nicaragua has a Marxist-Leninist regime, that is has been aiding insurgencies elsewhere in Central America, that domestic pluralism in Nicaragua has been greatly reduced and that Nicaragua has become a close ally of Cuba and the Soviet Union. The disagreement was no longer over the nature of the regime and its international alliances but what, precisely, to do about it.

Above and beyond this immediate debate, there was also widespread agreement in Washington, D.C., that the United States no longer could ignore Latin America, that it could no longer consider Latin America a second-rate area unworthy of serious and sustained attention. Latin America is not just important to the U.S. in a foreign policy sense but also because the area and its peoples are now intertwined with our domestic political considerations and constituencies and because the United States and Latin America are interdependent on a host of issues that had not been the case in the past (immigration, trade, investment, drugs, pollution, water resource, labor supplies, and markets).

The problem is that all these positive steps toward putting U.S. relations with Latin America on a more balanced, mature, and sophisticated basis may be submerged under current political preoccupations. It was the accepted wisdom in the nation's capitol that nothing much could get done in 1987 because of the Iran/Contragate issue and that little could be accomplished in 1988 because that was an election year. And of course little could be done in 1989 because it takes a year at least for a new administration to get organized.

The result was that not only were the positive accomplishments in Latin American relations of the last few years likely to be forgotten and not further implemented, but that in its preoccupation with domestic considerations the U.S. might have reverted de facto to a policy of benign neglect. That is a grave danger because it may well be argued that it was American benign neglect of Latin America in the 1970s—of Nicaragua, of El Salvador, of Guatemala, and of the rest of the hemisphere—that brought on the severe crisis the U.S. faced in that region at the end of the 1980s. Had the U.S. government dealt with Somoza in the early 1970s and responded strongly to the emergence of exceedingly repressive regimes in El Salvador and Guatemala around that same time—had the government not been preoccupied then with Vietnam and Watergate—it would not be facing the severe problems in the Caribbean area that have since come home to haunt and divide the country. Benign neglect is no longer a sound basis for U.S. policy in

Latin America, if it ever was, and it is not a policy (or the lack thereof) to which the U.S. can afford to return.

From Reagan to Bush

In the 1988 election campaign, candidate Michael Dukakis was perceived widely to be weak on defense and soft on communism. There is no doubt that the electorate preferred the Bush message of peace through strength as compared with Dukakis's foreign policy message which was thought by the voters to be wishy-washy. On Latin America, Dukakis seemed to prefer working through such moribund multilateral agencies as the Organization of American States; the candidate was also powerfully influenced by his experience in Latin America as a schoolboy during the U.S.-sponsored invasion of Guatemala in 1954. Dukakis' advisers told us that he still believed what he had learned, or thought he had learned, as a sophomore: that it is the CIA and the United Fruit Company who run Latin America. Clearly in 1989, thirty-five years later, such a belief was not at all a realistic picture of a region that has obviously become far more diverse and complex.

George Bush comes out of the moderate or centrist wing of the Republican Party. He is closer to the Eisenhower-Rockefeller-Nixon-Ford wing of the party than to the Goldwater-Reagan wing. All of his early appointments in the foreign policy area—James Baker at the State Department, William Webster at the Central Intelligence Agency, Brent Skowcroft at the National Security Council, Richard Chaney at the Department of Defense—were moderate Republicans, pragmatists rather than ideologues. But Bush also has to guard the political flanks on his right, so he cannot move policy too far away from the Reagan positions. In many areas Bush can be expected to continue the Reagan policies, meanwhile—on the debt as on Central America—nudging those policies in the direction of some greater pragmatism and centrism. But that of course is also what the Reagan administration was doing in its last few years: moving away from the extremes and increasingly toward the center. Once again the theme will be continuity in foreign policy, not dramatic reversals, although within this context there will be new faces and a nuanced policy.

Latin America does not appear to be a high priority in the Bush administration. As assistant secretary of state for inter-American affairs, a person was named who knows little Spanish and knows very little about the area. As one high State Department official told me, "He's totally unqualified for the job, and the best evidence for that is that he actually wants it!"

The one qualification this person did have is that he was a Democrat. The consensus is that what Secretary Baker wanted to do was to appease the congressional Democrats by appointing one of their own to the Latin America position. A policy will be hammered out—as on Nicaragua—that will also keep the congressional Democrats content- ed. Once Secretary Baker, through these means, has bought peace with the Congress on Central America, diffused the issue and gotten it off of the front pages, the calculus is that he would then be free to pursue his own policies on other, what are considered more important, foreign policy issues. It is clear in terms of both the personnel involved and the strategy being pursued that Latin America does not count for much, that once again the region is being used as a "throwaway" to buy greater political space on other issues deemed more important—NATO, dealing with the Soviets, disarmament. One may or may not agree with this assessment, but it clearly does not augur well for U.S.-Latin America policy. After the sometimes frenetic attention of the Reagan years, except perhaps for Mexico, we may be in for another period of benign neglect concerning Latin America.

Conclusions and Implications

We have seen that historically there has been a great deal of continuity in U.S. policy toward Latin America—more continuity than change, regardless of the party or president in control of the White House. American public opinion, interest groups, our system of checks and balances, and the force of international realties all tend to force American foreign policy back toward the middle, including in the administrations of Carter and Reagan, two of the most recent and more ideological presidents. The basic security goals of the United States in Latin America are set; the main questions for policy have centered on the best means to achieve these goals. We should not expect, therefore, any sudden or dramatic changes of policy from any new administration in Washington, despite campaign rhetoric to the contrary.

That is not to rule out change, however. The basics of policy may be set, but in any new administration there are new faces, new emphases, new ideas, and new initiatives. These nuances, within an overall context of policy continuity, provide room to maneuver and offer openings for new tilts of direction.

Moreover, some larger sea changes are also occurring in American attitudes and, hence, in American policy toward Latin America. In terms of immigration patterns and ethnic makeup, the United States is becoming something of a Caribbean nation. In some parts of the country the Hispanic vote has begun to affect domestic and, ultimately, international politics. As a nation, Americans are more aware of and somewhat better informed about Latin America than in the past. United States policy toward Latin America over the years, with certain notable "blips," has become more sophisticated and informed. It has begun to adjust to the new realities in Latin America and in inter-American relations. In recent years, there has been a learning curve whose general direction is upward on the part of all recent administrations, Congress, the media, and the general public, regarding Latin America.

The United States needs to continue along the lines of the general trends suggested here. Americans need a greater understanding of, and a greater sophistication regarding, Latin America. U.S. governments need a policy that is steady, positive, and long-term and not just reactive to crisis. They need less volatility in policies, and ones which do not elevate certain devils to an importance they may not deserve—be they authoritarian governments in one administration or "the Cubans" in another. Above all the United States needs sustained attention to Latin America and a consistent policy, rather than a situation of benign neglect which causes problems to fester to the exploding point, followed by a new period of crisis response and finger-pointing.

In short, the U.S. needs to put its relations with Latin America on the same sophisticated, mature, normal basis that it has long maintained with Western Europe. Such has been the general thrust of American foreign policy in recent years, despite the headlines which imply greater volatility and disagreement. Such a mature policy requires not only sustained attention to the area but, as all recent administrations have come to recognize, a balance of socioeconomic assistance and military aid, of strategic and human rights concerns, of promoting democratic development as well as U.S. security interests. Such a balanced and multifaceted policy is not only good in itself, but it also best serves the interests of both Latin America and the United States.

35

3

REAGAN, CENTRAL AMERICA, AND THE "CHART OF HISTORY"

Walter LaFeber

Perhaps the greatest of United States historians, and a classic conservative voice, Henry Adams, offered the following insight in his autobiography: "For history international relations are the only sure standards of movement, the only foundation of a map."[1] For this reason, Adams had always insisted that international relations was the only sure base for a chart of history.

If that passage is true, then the failure of the Reagan policies in Central America indicate that the chart of history has changed radically during the past decade, the map drastically altered. Within the lifetime of some who are still alive, Theodore Roosevelt arrogated to the United States the right to act as a policeman in the Caribbean-Central American region; he walked the beat of that neighborhood with his big stick. He moved U.S. forces around the Caribbean-Central American countries, created new governments, then publicly justified such use of power with his Roosevelt Corollary to the Monroe Doctrine—a corollary that gave the United States the responsibility for maintaining order in the region.[2]

The responsibility, however, soon demanded high expenditures. In 1912, U.S. troops began a twenty-year occupation of Nicaragua. Washington's interventionist policies produced at least twenty U.S military landings in the Caribbean-Central American region during those twenty years. By 1927, the troops had begun a six-year war against Nicaraguan guerrilla leader Augusto Sandino that, despite the ferocity of the fighting, failed to capture Sandino but did produce a Nicaragua under Anastasio Somoza and his sons with which North Americans

36

could live, with few regrets or twinges of conscience, for nearly a half-century.

Some observers were concerned. Another conservative voice, journalist Walter Lippmann, wrote in 1926 that Nicaragua was no longer "an independent republic . . . [and] the direction of its domestic and foreign affairs are determined not in Nicaragua but in Wall Street. . .. We continue to think of ourselves as a kind of great, peaceful Switzerland," Lippmann went on, "whereas we are in fact a great, expanding world power. . . . Our imperialism is more or less unconscious."[3] How conscious that expansion was remains a point of contention among scholars, but no one doubts Lippmann's assertion that "we are in fact a great, expanding world power," least of all Central Americans. As the head of the Honduran military reminded the U.S. ambassador to Tegucigalpa in the mid-1980s, Central Americans had good reason to believe the old axiom that as far as the United States was concerned, "its head was in Washington, its heart in England, and its feet in Central America."[4]

The Good Neighbor policy of Franklin D. Roosevelt made those feet less heavy in the 1930s and 1940s, but by the 1950s, the Good Neighbor, in the eyes of the U.S. officials, was no longer sufficient to keep the neighborhood orderly. When post-1944 changes in Guatemala produced a government in 1950 that decided it could improve the lot of its citizens (especially the majority of the citizenry, who were impoverished Indians) by expropriating property, and when that government moved to protect itself against growing U.S. pressure by accepting a shipment of arms from the Soviet bloc in the spring of 1954, the Central Intelligence Agency, with the aid of other Central Americans—most notably the Somoza dictatorship in Nicaragua—overthrew the Guatemalan government. That success proved short-lived. Not only did the U.S.-imposed government become one of the most vicious in the hemisphere over the next thirty years, but economic problems and revolutionary movements continued to multiply in the region. President John F. Kennedy's Alliance for Progress was supposed to help solve these problems and contain these post-Fidel Castro revolutionary movements by spending $100 billion over ten years in the 1960s to create a large, democratic, middle class in Latin America. After all, as Kennedy's advisers pointed out, Latin America already seemed to be going through a promising round of reform-minded, elected, governments that were replacing dictatorships; the Alliance for Progress could build on that strong foundation.

In perspective, we can now see that a number of democratic (or, more accurately, elected) regimes come into power in the region every fifteen to twenty-five years. Whichever U.S. president is in power at the time willingly takes credit for this turn of the cycle and proposes to build on it. In the 1960s, unfortunately, the Alliance for Progress did not build on, but helped wreck, the political foundation. The billions of dollars that poured into Latin America went largely into the hands of the richest people, not the poorest. After the so-called decade of development, as the 1960s were styled at the time, more revolutionary movements existed in Central America than when President Kennedy entered office in 1961.[5]

By mid-1979, one of the movements, that in Nicaragua, had captured power and another, in El Salvador, seemed about to do so. When U.S. officials tried to contain these movements in the late 1970s they discovered that—to use Henry Adams's phrase—the map had changed in Central America. The "standards of movement" had been altered since the time of the Roosevelts. The chart of history had changed the relationships in two respects particularly. First, U.S. unilateral action, which had dominated Nicaragua in the 1920s and Guatemala in the 1950s, no longer was an easy alternative for Washington officials. In the earlier days the United States had been able to remove governments by separating, often merely by buying off, the armies from the governments. After the Cuban revolution of 1959, however, such a separation was difficult to achieve. Fidel Castro had learned that when the government and the army were one (as he ensured they were at the Bay of Pigs in 1961), the United States had difficulty removing an unwanted government in the region.[6] By the 1980s, the only way to remove the Sandinista revolutionary government in Nicaragua was to destroy the Sandinista army, and that could not be accomplished without a costly invasion by United States (not merely U.S.-supported "contra") forces. The Rand Corporation told the Pentagon in the mid-1980s that such an invasion of Nicaragua would require 100,000 or more U.S. combat troops, and even then the job could "bog the United States down in a prolonged military occupation and counterinsurgency campaign." A military official in the U.S. Embassy in Managua believed it would require 150,000 to 200,000 troops to remain one and one-half to two years to pacify Nicaragua—assuming, of course, that U.S. domestic politics gave the Pentagon that much time to do the job. These estimates help explain why during the 1980s many of the uniformed military leaders in the Pentagon opposed using force to overthrow the Sandinistas, and why the U.S. military has worked against plans—usually devised by civilians within the U.S. government—to trigger a campaign against the Sandinistas that might require large numbers of U.S. troops to complete it successfully.[7]

The second change in Henry Adams's map was that the two Roosevelts at least had the compliance, if not the active help, of other Latin American nations in controlling disorder in the region. As late as 1965, President Lyndon Johnson even enjoyed strong support from the Organization of American States (OAS) and a number of individual Latin American governments in carrying out his policy of ensuring that an anti-Castro regime would hold power in the Dominican Republic after that nation exploded in disorder. In large part because of the 1965 experience, however, and because many Latin American nations believed they had been lied to by Johnson about the extent of the communist danger in the Dominican Republic, the OAS offered little help later to Presidents Jimmy Carter and Ronald Reagan in carrying out their policies. The OAS became an ignored organization, neglected by the United States because an automatic majority no longer was available to support U.S. policies, subordinated by Latin American countries that looked elsewhere for their security. Hemispheric cooperation degenerated into mutual suspicion and go-it-alone policies.

By 1988, the Reagan administration was virtually isolated in carrying out its Central American policies. Even as early as June 1979, when President Carter asked for OAS intervention to stop the Sandinistas from assuming power in Nicaragua, not a single other nation in the hemisphere would do so.[8] During the autumn of 1988, the United Nations General Assembly voted on a resolution asking that the United States comply with a World Court ruling that it (the United States) should pay for the damages caused by the CIA's attempt to blow up Nicaraguan harbor facilities and oil refineries in 1983-1984. The Reagan administration lobbied hard against the resolution, but the vote was 89 to 2 in favor of the measure; only the United States and Israel opposed the resolution. Forty-eight nations abstained. To claim, as did the Reagan administration, that other nations in the region wanted to continue to put pressure on the Sandinistas to democratize their system further and reduce Sandinista military strength was no doubt correct. But to claim that other Latin Americans, and especially Central Americans, wanted to use military power against the Sandinistas to achieve those goals was untrue. Central Americans wanted no expanded war that would kill more of their people, destroy more of their property

39

(or what was left to destroy in such devastated areas as El Salvador, Nicaragua, and much of Honduras), and pile on more debt in a region that already was crushed under one of the highest per capita debts of any part in the world.[9]

A great deal of multilateral diplomacy was carried on in Central America during the 1980s, but the most important—the Arias, or Esquipulas II, plan—tried to advance in 1987-1988 without much, if any, United States support.[10]   Indeed, the plan somehow managed to breathe, if barely, despite Secretary of State George Shultz's attempts in mid-1988 to work through Guatemalan and Costa Rican officials to condemn Nicaragua on the eve of the first anniversary meeting to assess the plan. "If we sign this statement," a Guatemalan official declared of the document Shultz wanted him to sign, "we are saying that our foreign policy is being set by the United States."[11]   Both countries (Costa Rica and Guatemala) said at the same time that they feared reprisals from Washington. Indeed, for some time the Reagan administration had been slowing down the provision of promised military aid to Guatemala and economic help for Costa Rica.[12]   Personally, U.S. officials actively disliked President Oscar Arias of Costa Rica as, perhaps, they had ever since 1986 when he refused their request to grant asylum in Costa Rica for deposed Philippine dictator Ferdinand Marcos. Josè Sorzano, of the National Security Council (NSC) in Washington, declared that in private White House officials "have a low opinion of [Arias] that borders on despising him. And," Soranzo continued, "Arias reciprocates. He has a low opinion of the Reagan administration."   One of Assistant Secretary of State Elliot Abrams's aides remarked that when Arias won the Nobel Prize for peace because of his Central American peace plan, "all of us who thought it was important to get aid for the contras reacted with disgust, unbridled disgust."[13]

But the contras could offer little hope to U.S. officials—and vice-versa.   Alfredo Cesar and four other former contra leaders announced in 1988 that they planned to return to Nicaragua to form a political party that would "struggle openly" to work for a political rather than a military settlement. In truth, the Reagan administration's attitude toward the contras had long been rather cynical. Publicly, the President termed the contras "freedom fighters," especially when Congress was debating contra aid. Privately, however, it was NSC Director Robert McFarlane, not a left-wing critic of the Reagan policies, who called the contras "well-meaning, patriotic, but inept Coca-Cola bottlers." (The Coca-Cola allusion referred to contra leader Adolfo Calero, who once owned the soft drink's franchise in Managua.) McFarlane continued: "They just cannot hack it on the battlefield."[14] The NSC Director's words went far in explaining why U.S. policy failed in Nicaragua.

But even in late 1988 as President Reagan offered to take responsibility for the 10,000 to 12,000 contra troops in Honduras (a responsibility which meant their possible resettlement in Central America or the United States), he and his successor, George Bush, hoped to keep open the possibility of using the contras as a political and military force to put pressure on the Sandinistas. Meanwhile, the National Endowment for Democracy, a private, congressionally funded nonprofit group, spent more than $800,000 in Nicaragua during 1987 to support the anti-Sandinista opposition. It pledged $2 million more to help anti-Sandinista candidates in the election planned for early 1990. The risk for the National Endowment for Democracy was that its recipients would appear to be mere hands and mouths of U.S. diplomacy. Both the endowment and the Nicaraguan recipients, however, were apparently willing to take that risk—not least because the internal Nicaraguan economic situation appeared so bleak that the Sandinistas seemed to be more vulnerable than ever before.[15] Expert observers returning from Nicaragua in 1988 reported that teachers told for the first time of children fainting in school classes because of lack of food. United States doctors working in Nicaragua, and sympathetic to the Sandinistas, reported that also for the first time since the 1979 revolution they were seeing numerous cases of malnutrition.[16] The devastation of the hurricane in 1988 only deepened the disaster. The Reagan administration refused to send U.S. government help or significantly bend the economic boycott it had imposed in 1985. The Sandinistas meanwhile refused to accept U.S. government aid for Nicaraguan children as long as the U.S. government also sent aid to the contra opposition. President Daniel Ortega declared that if the United States wanted to help, it could stop sending aid that was intended to "kill us." The Reagan administration also discouraged, albeit less successfully, the sending of aid from private U.S. organizations to Nicaragua.[17]

Into this breach stepped private U.S. groups who tried to move aid into Nicaragua despite the administration's economic blockade. In October 1988, a federal court judge in Houston sided with the private groups. He ruled that the president had no authority to regulate or prohibit donations of articles aimed at the relief of human suffering. The Veterans Peace Convoy, which had been waiting for the judge's ruling, then drove its thirty-eight vehicles legally across the U.S. border on their way to Nicaragua. No one could pretend that such private aid was sufficient to pump-prime the dried-up and mismanaged Nicaraguan economy; nor did the Eastern bloc and, especially, the Soviet Union, have the interest and/or the resources to provide the help needed by the Sandinistas. When Daniel Ortega visited Moscow in April 1985, Soviet leader Mikhail Gorbachev told him that the Soviets would continue to render friendly assistance to the Sandinistas, but the offer was not open-ended, nor had any Soviet official suggested that the USSR would aid the Nicaraguans with direct involvement in the event of a U.S. invasion.

During the first three quarters of 1988, Soviet arms shipments to Nicaragua fell about 17 percent in tonnage. Although the meaning of that drop can be debated, it seems likely that Gorbachev's government was reevaluating its entire relationship with revolutionary regimes in the newly emerging world. The Soviets were becoming much more interested in dealing with what they termed the rising industrial powers, such as Brazil and Argentina, than with the less-developed revolutionary nations. The Soviets assumed that although Latin America was of rising importance, the region was not vital to Moscow's interests. Even Robert Leiken, a scholar of the region who is not known as a warm friend of the Sandinistas, observed that "Moscow provides only enough military aid to make [any U.S.] military intervention costly and save the Soviet 'revolutionary reputation,'" but "not enough to guarantee [Sandinista] survival."[18]

If, then, one tries to measure the standards of movement in U.S.-Nicaraguan relations, it seems that any failure of Washington's policy in the region was not due to fear of a showdown with a Soviet-guaranteed Sandinista rule in Nicaragua, or to a diminishing of the U.S. military power in the region. President Reagan could have picked up a phone and set in motion power whose extent not even Theodore Roosevelt could have dreamed. The problem lay less in U.S. military abilities than in U.S. history, less in the North Americans' fear of the Soviet Union than in their fear of a revolution whose origins they still did not understand well enough to make that understanding a basis for U.S. policy, less in the decline of U.S. power than in the inability to calculate for what constructive ends the immense power of the United States could be used.

Washington's policy failures in Nicaragua were obvious to most observant Americans. That was one reason, no doubt, why polls continued to show in 1987 that a base of 60 to 70 percent of Americans opposed sending military aid to the contras.[19] The Reagan policy failure in El Salvador had been equally apparent, especially in 1988 as the revolutionaries of the Farabundo Marti National Liberation Front (FMLN) launched military attacks successfully into areas—including military sectors in the capital city of San Salvador—that Washington officials assumed were secure. The failure was also apparent when President José Napoleon Duarte left office in early 1989 with his reform program, and indeed his nation's economy, shattered. The failure was further apparent in the March 1989 election when Duarte's Christian Democratic Party was replaced by the right-wing Arena Party, some of whose members were linked to mass human rights atrocities, including the assassination of Archbishop Oscar Romero, who was murdered while saying mass in 1980. Meanwhile, atrocities by both the government-related death squads and the FMLN revolutionaries rapidly rose once again. One estimate had them at least doubling in number in 1988 after a decline in the mid-1980s. The Roman Catholic church in El Salvador and Mr. Duarte's own human rights commission expressed the fear of a return to the terror of the early 1980s.[20]

Many of these failures in U.S. policy toward El Salvador were apparent in 1988, as the Reagan administration prepared to leave office. But for those who cared to look, the U.S. failures had long been apparent. Perhaps the most remarkable public analysis anyone made of that post-1981 policy (and perhaps, as well, the most critical analysis made of that policy) was completed in the spring of 1988 by four lieutenant colonels in the United States Army who were specialists in the low-intensity-conflict strategy that developed during the 1980s. The four were also well acquainted with El Salvador. Their paper, entitled *American Military Policy in Small Wars: The Case of El Salvador*, had as its first author Lt. Col. A. J. Bacevich, and so, for brevity, it may be termed the Bacevich report.

The paper began by noting that "for the United States, El Salvador represents an experiment, an attempt to reverse the record of American failure in waging small wars, an effort to defeat an insurgency by providing training and material support without committing American troops to combat." The experiment, as the Bacevich report terms it, had taken sixty thousand lives and cost the United States $3 billion between 1978 and 1988. Over one hundred fifty U.S. military advisors (not the magic fifty-five number that was used to assure Congress of the limited direct U.S. involvement) worked in El Salvador, but the report nevertheless concluded that "the end of the war is nowhere in sight." It continued,

43

The FMLN—tough, competent, highly motivated—can sustain its current strategy indefinitely. . . . Despite important progress toward democratization, the Salvadoran government remains ineffective. By most estimates, the war in El Salvador is stuck; unhappily, the United States finds itself stuck with the war.

But the Bacevich report candidly stated that the very "progress toward democratization" surprisingly was part of the problem, not part of the solution. Elections in El Salvador were used by both the Reagan administration and Democratic-controlled Congresses to justify continued massive aid to the Salvadoran army. The Bacevich report, however, asked more fundamental questions about the very core of proclaimed U.S. policy:

Unfortunately making a government democratic does not make it effective. If anything, democratization has exacerbated the ineptness of the Salvadoran political system. At a time when war puts a premium on a single-minded, decisive governance, the opening up of Salvadoran politics has fueled partisanship and created conditions where nothing works. [One State Department official told us,] "Sometimes the worst thing you can do to defeat an insurgency is to nurture democratic institutions at the same time." The crux of the problem is that while building democracy implies dispersing power, waging war requires its concentration. This is an old notion, traceable at least back to Tocqueville.[21]

Perhaps Tocqueville was not read or remembered much in key sections of U.S. policy making, or, more likely, U.S. officials understood they faced a two-front war: elections in El Salvador that had to be held to show the U.S. Congress and a concerned public that the Central American nation was democratic and deserved support, and—on a second front—winning a bloody guerrilla war in the field. Congress and the public on the first front forced restraints on the war being waged on the second front. The irony was that both fronts of U.S. policy threatened to collapse. Washington's demands that Salvadorans become more liberal and humane were not sufficiently met. Nor was the Reagan administration's avowed policy of championing democracy consistent.

In 1982, when the right-wing Arena Party won the Salvadoran election, the United States intervened directly to prevent the winner from taking over the presidency. It was an odd way to demonstrate democratic procedure, but U.S. aid was more important to the survival of an anti-FMLN government than was such a procedure, and if Arena and its death-squad leaders had taken complete power, the United States Congress might well have shut off most aid. With massive help from Washington, Duarte and his Christian Democrats did win the 1984 election. In 1989, Arena, attacking the Christian Democrats' inability to stop either the war or the terrible economic decline, won with Alfredo Cristian as its presidential candidate. Roberto D'Aubuisson, the long-time power within Arena and closely linked to the terrorist death squads, remained sufficiently in the background so that most members of the U.S. Congress willingly continued to vote aid for the new government. Then Washington officials had little choice. El Salvador was so polarized that the only alternative to Arena was the FMLN. The democratic, moderate parties were only shells of their earlier power. As Ruben Zamora, a leader of the more moderate left, observed in 1988,

> The election itself is not going to solve the crisis in El Salvador. Already in the past seven years, we have had five general elections—more, I imagine, than any other country. And the crisis has not been solved; on the contrary, it is deeper now. Therefore, we have to be very clear that the election itself is not going to solve the problem.[22]

Political talks triggered by the Arias peace plan began between the star-crossed Duarte government and the FMLN, but they repeatedly broke down in 1987-1988, not least because the Salvadoran army, not Duarte, held ultimate power. That army would accept only a truce that forced the revolutionaries to lay down their arms.[23] As the Bacevich report repeatedly observed, the FMLN had no reason to lay down its arms. One could go farther: if Max Weber's dictum is true that a state is an entity that enjoys a monopoly of legitimate violence, then the Bacevich report substantiated many other observers who questioned whether Duarte's government was the real representative of the state.[24]

After more than a decade of war, El Salvador was bitterly divided and terrorism was on the rise. Honduras, the closest United States ally in the region, began to suffer from the same two characteristics. After obediently acting as the chief U.S. base in the region during the 1980s, Honduras, as Richard Millett observed in 1988, was "by almost every standard" worse off in 1987 than in 1981, "and the nation is less secure."[25] With at least forty thousand Nicaraguans, including as many as twelve thousand contra soldiers, forming virtually a separate nation in southern Honduras, and with the Hondurans' traditional and bitterest enemy—the Salvadorans—putting pressure along their common border, Hondurans began describing their nation as another Lebanon. Meanwhile, a draft U.S. treaty with Honduras was (according to the Honduran version) asking for permanent U.S. military bases to be built in Honduras, with North American aircraft and warships having the right to enter Honduran territory without permission from authorities in the capital of Tegucigalpa.

Perhaps the George Bush administration in Washington might provide an opportunity to rethink United States policies. If such a fundamental reassessment were to occur, and if Henry Adams's chart of history is kept in mind, the following might be concluded about the course of U.S. policy.

First, security interests have been further endangered, not protected, by the results of the Reagan policies in Nicaragua, El Salvador, and Honduras, and because U.S. officials refused to encourage actively and substantively the Arias plan for peace in the region. As Secretary of State George Shultz responded in 1988 when asked whether the United States should not have been involved in the diplomatic peace process much earlier, "You could argue that it might have been a good idea."[26] The Central Americans meanwhile had continued on their own way. As U.S. policies of military force helped destroy the region and threatened to expand the conflicts, the Central American leaders have tried to follow the paths of diplomacy and negotiated settlements that require compromise.

Second, the United States, over the long term and without using massive military power, has no longer been able to determine unilaterally how its perceived interests in the region can be protected. The era of Theodore Roosevelt lived briefly in the six-day war over Grenada, but no Grenadas exist in Central America.

Third, for one of the few times in recent U.S. history, public opinion—especially organized groups from churches and other groups that know about Central American affairs—played a major role in restraining U.S. power.[27] The attempt to circumvent that restraint, and thus the Constitution itself, led to the Iran-Contra scandal and the depths of the Reagan presidency. It reminded one of William Seward's warning 130 years earlier that slavery was evil not only because it enslaved blacks, but also because it corrupted whites. The political map, in other words, was being redrawn not only in Central America, where regional leaders following the policy of negotiated settlements were replacing Roosevelt's legacy of U.S. unilateral force, but in Washington itself where concerned and involved public groups shaped U.S. policy at the expense of executive power.

Samuel Goldwyn, the famous movie maker, supposedly once warned, "Never prophesy—especially about the future." But if an assessment such as this were to be held a half-century from now, it could be that the historians involved in the assessment would conclude that U.S.-Central American relations had reached a turning point in the decade 1978-1988. The larger question which that assessment would have to decide would be how well the sides had been able to follow the new lines on Henry Adams's chart and make the turn.

NOTES

1. Henry Adams, *The Education of Henry Adams. An Autobiography* (Boston: Houghton Mifflin, 1918), 422.

2. How the Roosevelt Corollary transformed the history of the Monroe Doctrine is argued in Walter LaFeber, "The Evolution of the Monroe Doctrine from Monroe to Reagan," in *Redefining the Past; Essays in Diplomatic History in Honor of William Appleman Williams*, ed. Lloyd C. Gardner (Corvallis, Oregon: Oregon State University Press, 1986), 121-41.

3. George Black, *The Good Neighbor* (New York: Pantheon, 1988), 45.

4. Roy Gutman, *Banana Diplomacy: The Making of American Policy in Nicaragua 1981-1987* (New York: Simon & Schuster, 1988), 105.

5. The effects of the Alliance for Progress on revolutionary movements are outlined and footnoted in Walter LaFeber, *Inevitable Revolutions: The United States in Central America* (New York: Norton, 1983), 111-26, 148-88.

6.   The effect of the 1954 Guatemala operation on Castro is well analyzed in Richard Immerman, *The CIA in Guatemala: The Foreign Policy of Intervention* (Austin: The University of Texas Press, 1982).

7.   Gutman, *Banana Diplomacy*, 277.

8.   J. I. Dominguez, ffiU.S. and its Regional Security Interests," *Daedalus* 109 (Fall, 1980): 116; Merilee Grindle, "Armed Intervention and U.S.-Latin American Relations," *Latin American Research Review* 16 (1981): 207-17.

9.   *Central America Report*, 31 Jan. 1986, 27; Eldon Kenworthy, "United States Policy in Central America," *Current History* 86 (Dec. 1987): 27.

10.   The text of the Arias plan can be found in the *New York Times* (*NYT*), 12 Aug. 1987, A8; for the 1989 agreement that established more specific criteria, especially for Nicaragua, see *NYT*, 16 Feb. 1989, A14.

11.   *NYT*, 31 July 1988, 1.

12.   *NYT*, 18 May 1987, A10; also Letters to the Editor in *NYT*, 12 Nov. 1987, A30.

13.   *NYT*, 7 Aug. 1988, 1, 14.

14.   Gutman, *Banana Diplomacy*, 341.

15.   The background is in the *Washington Post*, 19 March 1986, A1.

16.   Author's interview, October, 1988.

17.   *Washington Post*, 21 Sept. 1988, A28.

18.   Clifford Krauss, "Democracia," *Wilson Quarterly* (New Year's, 1988): 126; important background is in Peter Shearman, "The Soviet Challenge in Central America," in *Soviet Foreign Policy*, ed. Robbin F. Laird (New York: Academy of Political Science, 1987), 211-14; the Bush-Gorbachev

views of the Soviet-Central American relationship in early 1989 is in the *Washington Post*, 16 May 1989, A1.

19. A good analysis is in Morris J. Blachman and Kenneth E. Sharpe, "Central American Traps: Challenging the Reagan Agenda," *World Policy Journal* 5 (Winter 1987-1988): 25.

20. *Los Angeles Times*, 2 Oct. 1988, 6, reprinted in *Central America NewsPak*, 26 Sept.-9 Oct. 1988, 5.

21. Lt. Colonel A. J. Bacevich, et al., *American Military Policy in Small Wars: The Case of El Salvador*, John F. Kennedy School, March 1988 (manuscript), esp. 6-8, 91-94.

22. Ruben Zamora, "El Salvador After Duarte," *World Policy Journal*, 5/4 (1988): 117; also articles from *Excelsior* and the *Washington Post* in *Central America NewsPak*, 27 March-9 April 1989, 2-5.

23. Blachman and Sharpe, "Central American Traps,ff 16-17; Enrique A. Baloyra, "The Seven Plagues of El Salvador," *Current History* 86 (Dec. 1987): 415.

24. Weber is quoted by Yale Ferguson, "Analyzing Latin American Foreign Policies," *Latin America Research Review* 12 (3 Nov. 1987): 143.

25. Richard Millet, "The Honduran Dilemma," *Current History* 86 (Dec. 1987).

26. *New York Times*, 3 July 1988, 8.

27. Krauss, "Democracia," 131; Margaret Leahy, "The Harassment of Nicaraguanists and Fellow Travelers," in *Reagan Versus the Sandinistas: The Undeclared War on Nicaragua*, ed., Thomas W. Walker (Boulder, Colorado: Westview Press, 1987), 228-41; for important stories on the opposition of religious groups, see the *Washington Post*, 15 Aug. 1987, C12; 22 March 1986, C11.

4

COMMENTS, OBSERVATIONS, AND CONCLUSIONS
OF THE INTERNATIONAL VERIFICATION AND
FOLLOW-UP COMMISSION

The following is an unofficial translation of the previously leaked initial Spanish-language version of the "Comments, Observations, and Conclusions" of the International Verification and Follow-up Commission established by the Arias Peace Agreement. The commission's final report was watered down under heavy pressure from the United States and the Central American governments most closely tied with Washington. The document is included here as a substitute for the "off-the-record" comments of a member of the commission who addressed the symposium.

1. During their brief but informative visit to the region, the ad hoc representatives of the International Verification and Follow-up Commission for the Guatemala Procedure were witnesses to the Central American peoples' obvious yearning for peace; their longing for the establishment of regimes which, in addition to having been popularly elected, effectively guarantee the full exercise of human rights, economic development, and the dismantling of unjust, anachronistic social structures; and their fervent desire to control their own destiny, free from outside interferences and the East-West conflict. The peoples of Central American see themselves as the victims of a geopolitical conflict which does not concern them and of hegemonistic interests which are indifferent to their legitimate aspirations but determined to use them for their own ends.

2. In the hope of contributing to the achievement of these legitimate aspirations, which are the underlying rationale of the Esquipulas II commitments, the commission wishes to make the following detailed observations concerning fulfillment by the five Central American

governments of the commitments entered into in signing the Guatemala Procedure for the establishment of a firm and lasting peace in the region.

3. Despite some initial doubts, the five Central American countries have fulfilled the commitment, set forth in the Procedure, to set up National Reconciliation Commissions.

4. The five countries have not interpreted uniformly either the criteria governing the composition of the National Reconciliation Commissions or their method of decision making. It would be advisable if the difficulties which have emerged could be resolved on the basis of the comments made in the paragraphs that follow.

5. In the spirit of reconciliation on which the Procedure is based, it would have been desirable, particularly in those countries "where deep divisions have come about within society," for the National Reconciliation Commissions to include representatives of political parties or groupings close to irregular forces or insurrectionist movements. This has been done only in the case in Nicaragua. Where it has not been done, the reconciliation functions of the National Reconciliation Commission have been impaired.

6. In the case of El Salvador, withdrawal from the National Reconciliation Commission by several of its members, including the two representatives of opposition political parties, has created an unforseen situation which casts doubts on the commission's ability to fulfill the tasks set forth in the Procedure.

7. In the case of Nicaragua, the desire to take decisions by consensus appears to have prevented the National Reconciliation Commission from performing the verification functions provided for in section 1 (c) of the Procedure.

8. El Salvador, Guatemala, Honduras, and Nicaragua have issued amnesty decrees, despite the reservations expressed by Honduras as to whether the commitment was applicable to it. In the case of Costa Rica, the commission believes that the issuance of an amnesty decree would assist the overall peace effort, regardless of whether the amnesty provisions of the Procedure are applicable to Costa Rica and notwithstanding the fact that there is no government policy of political persecution there.

9. With regard to the content and scope of the decrees, criticisms were heard in some cases. In the specific case of El Salvador, the commission found that the amnesty decree had pardoned those allegedly responsible for the deaths of large numbers of people but

had given armed insurgents only fifteen days in which to avail themselves of the amnesty. It is hard to see how an amnesty thus conceived could assist the national reconciliation process.

10. In the case of Nicaragua, the entry into force of the amnesty decree has been made contingent on certification by the International Verification and Follow-up Commission that states of the region and from outside the region have fulfilled the commitment to terminate aid to irregular forces and to prevent their territory from being used to attack Nicaragua. This invoking of the principle of simultaneity of commitments is one of the structural problems of implementing the Procedure which are discussed below.

11. In reviewing the number of political prisoners in each country who might have availed themselves of the amnesty, the commission heard important testimony in El Salvador, Guatemala, and Honduras to the effect that, to varying degrees, it had been systematic practice to physically eliminate captured members of irregular groups or insurrectionist forces.

12. It must be borne in mind that the purpose of the amnesty was to open up a political space in each country so that opposition groups, particularly armed insurgents, might return to democratic life. It is therefore premature to make a final judgment as to the effectiveness of the amnesty decrees as an instrument of national reconciliation.

13. Since the democratization envisaged in section 3 of the Guatemala Procedure embodies standards and practices which few countries in the world have attained, it is not difficult to see why it has not been achieved in five short months in a region with a turbulent history and little democratic tradition.

14. It is fair to recognize the stability and extensive development of democratic institutions in Costa Rica, although some sectors of society believe that the prevalence of a traditional two-party system does not permit the necessary degree of popular participation.

15. In the case of Nicaragua, the commission found that, despite the seriousness of the belligerent harassment to which the country is being subjected, tangible steps have been taken to set in motion a democratic process. However, it did hear the view expressed that a clearer differentiation would have to be made between state institutions and party institutions and that broader guarantees would have to be established for the exercise of democratic rights.

16. According to the vast majority of sources of information consulted, attempts by the heads of state of these countries to promote effective

participation in democratic life by the various currents of opinion and to ensure the protection of human rights are being hampered by the inability of democratically established authorities to exert due control over the state security apparatus, and by the action of military, security and paramilitary groups.

17. The commission was able to see that there is no state of siege or emergency in force in Costa Rica, El Salvador, Guatemala, or Honduras. In El Salvador, however, a decree-law issued following the lifting of the state of siege and still in force grants powers of detention which are essentially the same as those existing under the state of siege. In Nicaragua, the lifting of the state of emergency is subject to the same conditions as the entry into force of the amnesty decree. In practice, the state of emergency is applied with a degree of flexibility. In more than one country, the fact that the remedy of *amparo*, or *habeas corpus*, cannot be invoked in practice means that people often are detained for longer periods and in less favorable conditions that those envisaged by law.

18. The commission has followed with satisfaction preparations in the five countries for the establishment of the Central American Parliament. The creation of this important institution will be a significant step forward in the democratization process and will strengthen political, economic, and social integration among the countries of the region.

19. The failure to reach cease-fire agreements in the countries in which there are armed conflicts, and the intensification of these conflicts following the signing of Esquipulas II, with the resulting loss of life and material damage, are cause for justified and constant concern.

20. Moreover, in El Salvador, Guatemala, and Nicaragua, appeals to irregular forces or insurrectionist movements to agree to a cease-fire, avail themselves of the amnesty, and join in the political process in their respective countries, as envisaged in the Guatemala Procedure, have been unsuccessful. The commission is convinced that the efforts at dialogue and negotiation which those three countries and Honduras must make with a view to national reconciliation need to be pursued and intensified.

21. Despite the appeals made by the Central American presidents, it remains the policy and practice of the United States government to provide assistance, particularly military assistance, to irregular forces operating against the government of Nicaragua. The definitive termination of such assistance is still an indispensable

53

prerequisite for the success of peace efforts and the success of the Procedure as a whole.

22. From the testimony received, the commission believes that the commitment not to use the territory of one state to attack another has not been fulfilled. Reports have been received from some governments in the region concerning assistance to irregular forces and insurrectionist movements allegedly provided by other Central American governments, and concerning the use of the territory of some states for attacks on others. In this connection, complaints have been lodged by El Salvador against Nicaragua, and by Nicaragua against Honduras, El Salvador, and Costa Rica. The commission is not in a position to verify the reports, since it has so far been unable to set up on-site inspection mechanisms. It must point out that the use of the territory of states of the region for attacks on other states, with or without the consent of the government whose territory is involved, facilitates the operations of aforementioned forces and movements and makes it difficult to achieve a cease-fire.

23. With regard to refugees, the commission noted with satisfaction that progress has been made both in the establishment of institutional mechanisms and in such specific areas as protection, assistance, and voluntary repatriation. This clearly represents a step forward in the search for humanitarian solutions to the problems of the region. In this connection, the holding, during this year, of an international conference on Central American refugees, under the auspice of the governments of the countries of the region and with the cooperation of the Office of the United Nations High Commissioner for Refugees, would be a significant contribution to peace efforts.

24. The underlying strategy of Esquipulas II—to secure the cessation of hostilities through a broad amnesty, democratization, termination of aid for irregular forces and insurrectionist movements, and nonuse of territory to attack other states—has not been achieved to date. The fact that the desired objective has not been achieved does not, however, invalidate the strategy, although there must be permanent political will to seek ways and means of overcoming the obstacles.

25. In evaluating the progress made in implementing the Procedure for the establishment of a firm and lasting peace in Central America, signed at Guatemala City on 7 August 1987, it is essential to bear in mind that, as its title suggests, the Procedure constitutes a program of actions that are part of a process. Accordingly, 150

days after the signing of the agreement, it would be just as untrue to say that it has failed as to declare it a success, something which would, moreover, be premature.

26. It must be remembered that, just as Central America's political, economic and social structures did not deteriorate suddenly, so too peace in the region cannot be achieved overnight. The factors at play are by nature complex and operate at different levels at the same time. Several of the actors on the Central American stage are not parties to the agreement signed by those primarily concerned, namely, the heads of state of the region. The challenge of implementing it is therefore enormous; it does not seem realistic to expect a comprehensive, universally satisfactory, simultaneously implementable and verifiable agreement, and one which also commits and binds parties that are engaged in the short term. The task at this stage is not therefore to declare an ongoing process a success or a failure but to assess the progress made, identify the work that remains to be done, and suggest ways of proceeding with it.

27. For these reasons, the commission, having referred to the specific elements of its mandate, feels a need to make two general observations, not only because they affects its own responsibilities but also because they have a bearing on the broader question of compliance with the Procedure as a whole by its signatories.

Verification

28. It should be noted that several members of the commission have expressed concern about the participation of the Central American countries, as parties to a conflict, in the verification process. At commission meetings, there was obvious concern that this situation might undermine the credibility and effectiveness of verification. At the commission's fourth meeting, a first step was taken towards overcoming this problem. It was agreed that, in drafting the conclusions of the commission's report to the five Central American presidents, when conclusions were drafted concerning individual Central American countries, the representative of the country concerned would be able to state his position if he did not agree with them. The presidents could consider this matter at their next meeting in order to draw a practical distinction between Central American commission member and non-Central American commission member participation, with regard to verification proper, in

order to ensure that the verification process is completely impartial, objective, and effective. Strictly speaking, this would not require any tampering with the letter of this Procedure. This matter is also related to another problem which could be sensed during the commission's meeting, that is, the lack of a more precise framework for decision-making.

29. One of the first points considered by the commission was the need to work out practical arrangements for verifying the agreements set forth in the Guatemala Procedure. For verification of the commitments undertaken with the regard to security, that is, a cease-fire, non-use of territory to attack other states, and termination of aid for irregular forces and insurrectionist movements, on-site inspection is a sine qua non for any process of verification that is to be objective, independent, and effective. All members of the commission accept this basic premise and no one questions the need for such a mechanism to be duly established in order for the commission to initiate the process of verification and follow-up.

30. The commission is pleased to note that, since its fourth meeting, the obstacles encountered by the United Nations/OAS preliminary technical mission appear to have been surmounted. Accordingly, member governments agree to request the secretary-general of the United Nations and the secretary-general of the Organization of American States to send, as a matter of urgency, a further technical mission to the region to finalize the details for the establishment in the five Central American countries of mobile units with the characteristics outlined in the mission's second report.

Simultaneity and Reciprocity: Need for an Implementation Plan

31. The commission considers it relevant to point out that there are other, structural factors which might affect the implementation of the Procedure as a whole. These factors are as follows:

32. The distinctive feature of Esquipulas II lies less in formal legal obligations than in the political commitment on which the agreement is based and in the indisputable fact that it enjoys broad popular support and unanimous international support which give it legitimacy.

33. Nevertheless, the Procedure lacks some of the elements that normally make the practical application of peace agreements easier.

56

It is a unique document, similar in ways to a law without implementing provisions. It contains no implementation plan or practical timetable for the fulfillment of commitments. What section II establishes is a program of compliance proper, and a timetable for the verification and follow-up of compliance; this does not make up for the omission.

34. By now, it is more or less public knowledge that what permitted agreement on the Guatemala Procedure was that the differences among the parties regarding the sequence for the fulfillment for the different commitments were resolved when it was agreed that commitments should be fulfilled simultaneously. The international community warmly welcomed this formula, which settled apparently irreconcilable differences concerning the central problem of precedence between peace-making and democratization.

35. The differences of opinion, precisely on the sequence of actions, have made it all too apparent that simultaneous fulfillment cannot be achieved in practice unless it is clearly defined. This is a substantive and urgent problem. The document on simultaneity adopted by the executive commission represents a commendable effort to solve the problem on a theoretical level, but it does not solve the problem on a practical level. Rather, it continues to evade it.

36. The reluctance to tackle this problem is, of course, understandable; the development of an orderly, chronological plan for the implementation of the Procedure calls for negotiations.

37. This complex test, which involves an element of risk but is inescapable, could be given a decisive boost on the occasion of the return to the source offered by the San José meeting of the Central American presidents. Such negotiations require the opening up and, to some extent, the prizing apart of the delicate framework of the agreement of the executive commission. The presidents might consider the possibility of interpreting the concept of simultaneity in a way that made it less rigid. To give an example, actions as dissimilar as cease-fires and elections clearly cannot be implemented on a strictly simultaneous basis. The Procedure itself sets different dates for these actions, thereby automatically derogating from the principle of strict simultaneity.

38. As a result, would it not be better to interpret simultaneity as referring instead to the launching of the Procedure, that is, the fixing of the date from which commitments become reciprocally

binding? The commission dares to suggest that the time has come to emphasize reciprocity as the key to solving the problem of simultaneity.

39. Starting from an agreement that as of 5 November 1987 the commitments contained in the Guatemala Procedure simultaneously became reciprocally binding, it would be possible to design an implementation plan which was not tied to single peremptory date.

40. The increased room for maneuver that this would provide would even make it possible to draw up more manageable subplans or minipackages. Some governments' fear of taking action when another government has not taken the action would be overcome by the fact that any individual action would ultimately be subordinated to compliance with the whole.

5

GOVERNOR RICHARD CELESTE'S POSITION ON THE TRAINING OF OHIO NATIONAL GUARDSMEN IN HONDURAS

Carolyn J. Lukensmeyer

I am really pleased to be here with you tonight, and honored to share the podium with Manuel Rodríguez Arriaga and Alejandro Bendaña, and I am sorry that I did not hear your presentations this afternoon.

I have to admit, I want to approach this evening with a great deal of humility. I am sure that most people in this room are in many ways more schooled than I, and have a more detailed perspective of many of the policy issues in Central American than I do at the moment. Frankly, based on my discussions with them, I am going to change how I was going to do this a little bit. I would like to tell you what I want to accomplish, and then I may move back and forth between a kind of straight speech and some dialogue with you folks.

Given what I learned about the program in which you are participating, and what you have already been through today, I think there are three things of value for me to explore with you. Basically, these three things make up the background—and will provide some understanding of—the key issues that formed the governor's [Richard F. Celeste, Ohio governor, 1983-1991] policy position of deciding *not* to support the training of Ohio National Guardsmen in Honduras. I am sure what I will struggle with is not to give you too much detail, but instead give you some breadth, some perspective on how we arrived at that position. Equally important, I think, is some insight into the actions that actually occurred, and the four stages on which they occurred: the governor's office itself; the U.S. Congress; the governor's trip to

59

Honduras in mid-1987; and the U.S. court actions that took place regarding this issue at the same time.

I look forward to the opportunity for candid discussion about this inside view of what it means when a governor chooses to put himself in a policy position that is in opposition to a position of a federal government; how that plays itself out in the decision process; what actions are taken and what reactions have to be considered; and, finally, what kinds of tools are brought to bear to make it difficult for a governor to do that. I will be as candid as is appropriate for the circumstances. Once I get started I may make it hard to interrupt, but this is an open invitation on my part for you to do so.

On 1 April of this year [1988], an advance team of eleven Ohio National Guardsmen left Dayton, Ohio, for the Yoro Province in Honduras to prepare for military maneuvers. Dubbed by the Pentagon "Blazing Trails '89," the full operation was to begin in about six months. That flight of the eleven young Ohioans, members of our Guard's 16th Engineering Brigade, tangibly symbolized an inevitable blow to the Celeste administration's position in a two-year battle opposing the training and involvement of guardsmen in active strike areas in Central America.

That battle began in May of 1986 when the governor withdrew his approval of assigning guardsmen to a country adjacent to Nicaragua. At the time, that controversy appeared very straightforward. The U.S. Department of Defense, through the National Guard Bureau, has a program called the Overseas Deployment Training Program, and it planned to send Ohio National Guardsmen to rural Honduras to train and build roads. This was no different from several other missions which had sent Ohioans to Central America over a long period of time.

Governor Celeste, as commander in chief of the Ohio National Guard, and a vocal critic of U.S. policy in several Central American countries, was fearful of sending Ohio into a country bordering a nation embroiled in civil war, and he clearly opposed Ohio's military involvement in the region.

When he made that choice in May of 1986, it seemed to be a classic case of states' rights versus federal rights. It evolved into a challenge that governors are rarely asked to face. It became a challenge not just of crossing Ohio's borders to impact national policy, but of crossing America's borders to impact and influence our country's foreign policy. The governor's decision placed him in the position of making not just a bold statement about upholding states' rights, but what was perceived as a threatening, radical, and inappropriate statement from a governor about foreign policy.

Four major factors influenced the evolution and development of the governor's policy position as he faced the challenge of communicating from the Statehouse to the White House. The four levels of concern were the following: first, the role and purpose of the National Guard, from a historical perspective; second, the safety and well-being of the troops, the Ohio National Guardsmen themselves; third, the governor's judgment on the—intended or unintended, but nonetheless *physical*—consequences of the Reagan policy of intervention in Central America on economic development; and, last, what I acknowledged already, Governor Celeste's personal strong feelings about what is necessary for peace to evolve in Central America.

I would like to talk first about the role and purpose of the National Guard. This was, frankly, one of the largest surprises to me when I moved from being a private citizen to what would have been a rather hot position in any governor's administration. Since 1974, the role of the National Guard in this country has changed dramatically. Article 1, Section 8 of the U.S. Constitution created the state militia, completely commanded by governors during peacetime, yet able to be called up by the president to serve the U.S. military during times of war or national emergency.

It was in 1903 that those state militias, as individual units, were transformed in an amendment to the National Defense Act into what we came to know as the National Guard. A key principle was still underlined and maintained: that the individual state units of the National Guard were under the complete command of governors *unless* there was a circumstance of wartime or a national emergency. Basically, this constitutional purpose maintained itself for almost two hundred years. What changed it was the war in Vietnam. Between 1972 and 1974, the combined branches of the military faced an unprecedented average 34 percent decline in peacetime enlistment. Clearly, one of the tragic consequences of our involvement in the Vietnamese War was the way in which it debilitated, on many levels, the stature, the efficiency, and the effectiveness of the armed services in this country.

In responding to concerns about whether or not we would have a sufficient number of young men and women in the armed services without going back to conscription, in 1974 Congress passed a law that enabled us—for purposes of national security readiness—to *shift* the primary role of the National Guard. It was this act of Congress in 1974

61

that raised the constitutional question of a governor's commander in chief role in the National Guard versus the Defense Department's role—acting through the National Guard Bureau—with the National Guard.

The act was called the Total Force Policy: it is outlined in a briefing I received in February of 1987. (I think it is worth noting here that we were virtually the *last* of the fifty states to be briefed on the Defense Department's latest version of what number of troops were to go where for what purposes.) In February, I sat in on a portion of that briefing. As a person who had traveled a lot around the world, and who had been to some of the locations in Latin America, I found the briefing a frightening experience. Essentially, this act of Congress allowed National Guardsmen to be trained in foreign countries under the auspices of the training exercises sponsored by the U.S. Defense Department on behalf of the state.

The exercises were purported to be, and in large part are, goodwill efforts related to economic development projects such as the building of roads and airstrips. Now again, neither myself nor Governor Celeste would challenge the fundamental value of training troops that are part of the armed forces strategic strike force. If, indeed, this country became involved in conventional warfare again, the National Guard is where we would look for a surprising percentage of the ground forces and personnel forces to be engaged in battle.

By definition, then, those forces should be trained on the most sophisticated equipment and the most sophisticated technology. They should have the opportunity for training *on site* in a variety of locations. I did not happen to put in these notes that the number of places around the world where this training goes on is, I believe, above forty, so the Defense Department has many options about where to send the National Guard for this on-site training.

The issue that Governor Celeste was raising is the *percentage* of the training that today is taking place in Central America, particularly in Honduras. Why are we not asking the obvious question? Why in an area of the world where there is an existing strike, conflagration, actual war—whatever the issue may be—do we have a large presence of American troops supposedly only for training purposes adjacent to that area?

No state had challenged the constitutionality issue over peacetime gubernatorial control of the National Guard between 1974, when this act was enacted, and 1986—despite the fact that the Reagan administration had increased and shifted the location of this training to a dominance in Central America at the beginning of 1982. In May of 1986, Celeste became the first governor to make such a challenge when he withdrew blanket approval for sending Ohio National Guardsmen to any countries selected by the Pentagon. From the time the governor took office in 1983 until his decision in 1986, sixteen thousand Ohio guardsmen had participated in overseas development training programs, about 80 percent of them in Central America.

Until May of 1986, the phrase "blanket approval" essentially meant that the commander in chief of the Ohio group (who happens to be a gentleman named General Temple) would send an "orders" telegram, which actually is a national security document, to the adjutant general of the Ohio Guard. Other than an information link back into the governor's office, by definition those troops just went wherever they were assigned, whenever they were assigned.

This was being tracked very carefully in the governor's office. Then in May of 1986, Governor Celeste announced to General Temple that he wanted personal review of where the troops would be sent and for what purposes. Based on his understanding of the governor's role, and based on the fact that this was not a war, nor a national emergency, he felt that this information was absolutely necessary for him to make a gubernatorial decision before he signed off on sending those troops.

Within a few weeks of that announcement, the adjutant general of the state of Ohio received the first of a series of interactions that went on for more than a year of threats—sometimes direct and sometimes veiled—of the cutoff of funds for equipment, cutoff of funds for training, cutoff of funds for specific bases in Ohio. Essentially the message was, "If Ohio will not play its role in blanket approval of where the troops should be sent, it will lose federal dollars invested in the state."

Now again, I have no notion of how much you are aware of the role the National Guard plays in education, but for a very large percentage of certain classes and geographic distribution of people, the National Guard today is one of the main ways in which young people get educated, not just in Ohio but all over America. The tuition scholarship grants that are available to the National Guard are a prime motivation for many people to join the guard. So a threatened reduction of funds—either bases or equipment or personnel—is a rather significant retaliatory action against a governor for announcing an intention to be in the decision loop about where Ohio National Guardsmen will be deployed.

Let me stop here and see if you have any questions, or if there is a discussion, before I move to one of the other four issues that formed the governor's policy.

Q: What are the governors who are in opposition to this policy losing?

A: I was going to get into that a little later, because it raises broad questions, but I will address it now. Rudy Perpich, governor of Minnesota, took a strong leadership position in filing suit against the Montgomery amendment that passed Congress sometime in 1987. Twelve states joined Governor Perpich in filing that suit against the Montgomery amendment and, I am sure, similar tactics of retaliation evolved over time. Seven of those twelve states dropped out of that suit, and in the end only five states supported Governor Perpich's stance.

In 1986, when Governor Celeste literally refused to allow guardsmen to be assigned, he was the only governor doing so. But in April of this year, when our 16th Engineering Brigade went to Honduras, Governor Celeste had, in fact, complied. The difference is that when we did that in 1986, the Montgomery amendment appeal had not taken place. We said that we would comply with whatever the outcome of the Perpich suit was. So at this point there are no governors who have not, in the end, actually allowed troops to be sent.

Q: What "chits," what resources, did the governor have in case of a showdown? We're talking about consequences. What did he have going for him?

A: Well, it was not exactly a fair fight!

Q: Do you know, did he have anything in his corner?

A: Actually, I do. I said this lightly and in a good humor. One of the "chits" was box tickets to an Ohio State football game! General Temple is from Ohio and wanted very much to see a game. In fact, I am not only kidding. . . . One of the things about holding a job like this is you learn a little too much about how the world works.

As you know we were faced with certain dilemmas. What allowed us to go as far as we went in a confrontation stance was the suit challenging the Montgomery amendment. As people in this audience probably know, the Montgomery amendment was upheld, so the congressional act took precedence. It affirmed national federal rights over states' rights. Perpich and the five governors who stayed with it are still appealing that process, which we all know could go on for a long time, but we fought back by linking Senator Metzenbaum in. Senator Glenn also has been terrific in terms of his strong support, the role he plays in the key committees in the Senate, and how much he is respected in the Pentagon. So it was a communication, but informal—"chits" was your word—rather than there being anything for the governor to really fall back on.

Q: At what level was Perpich's court action, in terms of jurisdiction?
A: This was in the U.S. District Court, 5 August 1987. However, the judge concluded that the congressional act would stay. It has been appealed to the federal court above that. I apologize that I cannot give you the number of it. I will find that out and get back to you. It has been sitting there for quite a while. Governor Dukakis filed an additional process in the meantime. The Dukakis filing also has been dropped, so the only current activity in the court is the appeal of the Perpich suit.
Q: Presumably that would continue all the way up to the Supreme Court?
A: I think so. The five governors are staying with it. Governor Celeste will certainly stay with it. I am convinced that Governor Perpich will also.
Q: As far as you know it is not on the Court's docket.
A: It is not on the Court's docket.

Let me go back to the next item that I said was a key focus for the governor: the issue of the safety of the troops. Since the U.S. buildup began in Central America about six years ago, some fifty-five thousand National Guardsmen have passed through Honduras in training exercises, mostly of the type which I have described to you: engineering brigades, and survey brigades. No National Guard troops have been involved in combat exercises. However, some members of the armed services and reserve guard services have been involved in combat exercises. So one of the things that we tracked very carefully each time an Ohio group was sent was detailed observations by an independent member—someone not a member of the brigade that was going. That person reports directly to Governor Celeste as to whether there is any overlap, any abuse in terms of shifting our guardsmen from, say, engineering survey activity into combat training. Getting back to your question, we feel that in terms of where we have positioned ourselves—with Secretary Carlucci in the Defense Department, with Temple in the National Guard Bureau—about the only thing we can do is call foul play if, indeed, any guardsman is used beyond what is in the stated purpose of training guardsmen around the world.

This past March, when Secretary of State Schultz did the high-risk flex of military muscle—Operation Golden Pheasant, in which thirty-two hundred U.S. troops went to Honduras to counter the invasion of Nicaraguan soldiers battling retreating contra rebels in Honduras—we upped the ante again. An additional letter went to Defense Secretary Carlucci restating the issues we had raised when we returned from Honduras in 1987, and reestablishing the same rationale that Governor Celeste had suggested before: that it was unsafe and provocative to have such a large presence of American troops there, whether they were active soldiers or National Guardsmen.

An example of how the safety issue affected guardsmen who were not involved in active combat occurred around the time Governor Celeste visited Honduras in July of 1987. At that time three marines died from a sabotage attempt in a local restaurant. As I mentioned before, forty American military personnel have been killed in Honduras since 1983 when this buildup began. And although each of the forty incidents was by itself an isolated event not directly related to combat, nonetheless, that is a pretty shocking figure in terms of what is supposed to be a training exercise.

The position that the governor took in terms of the threatened safety and well-being of the guardsmen was that strong military buildup and sustained training exercises of whatever nature *by definition* evoke aggression and raise questions about the role and purpose of the United States government in these exercises. He has stated this in writing to the president, in writing to National Guard Bureau, and verbally several times to Defense Secretary Carlucci: that by definition, the risk factor is there for any guardsman who is sent to Honduras, simply because of the highly visible, large numbers of American military.

The governor substantiated for himself what we had suspected would be true after the very sophisticated briefing the national policy advisors and people from the Defense Department had with the governor before he went to Honduras. The Honduran military definitely wants this large American presence. There is no question about that, about what it has done for the Honduran military in terms of access to equipment and in terms of access to new training techniques—not just for civilian support services, but for actual combat.

The governor met with several of those people on the Honduran trip, and they are highly sophisticated, upper-level personnel, many of whom have advanced degrees in U.S universities, many of whom emulate the U.S. military and would like to be part of it. So there is no question from a policy perspective that what the U.S. is doing there can be justified easily in terms of the invitation from the Honduran government and the Honduran military.

Governor Celeste strongly feels that when there are alternative training opportunities, those should be used. Why would we send people to an area where forty people have died in seven years, where there is a risk of actual contact in a combat situation? Why are not those troops deployed in one of the other thirty-seven or forty-two training places around the world? Again, we are keeping the distinction between the use of the National Guard versus troops that are in the Army or Army Reserves. The point is not necessarily combat readiness—except in the big picture, of course. The point is what we are being told is the purpose of the guard: economic development and infrastructure support (road building and bridge building).

(Someone in the audience said, "We could use them in southern Ohio to build us some bridges and make some roads . . . and leave some of the equipment for us!" Lukensmeyer replied, "People are going to think I paid you to say that! I will get to the economic development issue in a few minutes.")

Let me say one more thing about the politics of this for the governor in early 1987, when it was clear that he was going to hold his ground. For many Ohio National Guardsmen, the opportunity to go to another country for a training experience is very, very attractive. So we put a lot of time and energy into direct contact between the governor and the leadership of the officers of the Ohio National Guard. This included "town meetings" with members of the guard. We made a point of this because there is a great deal of static involved in being in one of the units selected to go on these international training missions.

As they followed the developments of the governor's position through the media, we received from the public enormous support on the issue of the safety and well-being of the guardsmen. From guardsmen themselves, however, we were receiving a great deal of criticism. Many units had been in Central America. They had *not* experienced a problem; in fact, they came back talking about what a great experience it is to be in the jungles of Honduras. Now, if you have never been any place outside of America, you all know that your first experience internationally is an eye-opener, whatever the circumstances. So before Governor Celeste went to Honduras in July of 1987, we made a special point of being available to dialogue and talk with guardsmen themselves, both men and women, both officers and enlistees. We made a point of really exploring the issue so that they would understand his policy position, so that they would not be informed only by what they read in the newspaper, but would have a chance to understand his judgment of their safety and well-being, his judgment on the purpose of the guard, his judgment on economic development, and his judgment on U.S. foreign policy.

My guess is that is a very atypical stance for a governor to take: spending the time and energy, not just to deal with developing a position, but to keep that an evergreen, interactive process for the people whose lives were being impacted. We know that we did influence some guardsmen in that respect. But I do not know what the vote would be today if you asked the Ohio guardsmen whether they still support Governor Celeste's position on this, or whether they believe they should be allowed to go train in places the National Guard Bureau wants to send them. I do not know the answer to that question.

Let me shift to the economic development question. As many of you know, Governor Celeste was the director of the Peace Corps under President Carter. He used that experience very well in terms of his own global education, visiting almost 130 countries during that time. A major focus of his visit was going to those countries where Peace Corps volunteers have been for many years to track how the technology transfer had or had not impacted economic development. So Governor Celeste is a governor with very strong feelings about the role of the United States in the economic development of developing countries.

As you asked, sir, "What's wrong with the National Guard helping build roads?" We all know there is not a community or state in this country that does not have serious infrastructure problems. Why would we not do that at home as well as allowing it to be done abroad?

There is a very real, fundamental reason: it is illegal in the United States of America. It is illegal because using the National Guard for construction work, by definition, takes jobs away from citizens. That phenomenon is exactly what is happening in Honduras. It manifests itself in two specific ways.

First, there are large questions about the roads and bridges that are being built in the Yoro Province, where Governor Celeste went in 1987. The roads that our troops were working on at that time had been started more than three times during a six-year period. You could actually see the erosion, the lack of maintenance. They were built high in the mountains in areas where, again, the farm market link is highly questionable. It is questionable as to whether the road exists in that area for any purpose other than allowing travel over previously inaccessible areas of high mountains not that far from the border.

Second, in terms of economic development, is the issue of *how* we are doing this. We are doing it with equipment flown into the country with our National Guardsmen and flown out of the country when our units leave. Other than some Honduran military, there is no attempt to train any local people or to even *use* local people in the road construction and the bridge building processes. So we are spending virtually hundreds of thousands of dollars in men and equipment to go in to work on infrastructure where no technology transfer is being done with local people and no equipment is even left behind. We believe that most of what has been done in Honduras since 1983, once we decide to stop intervening in this way, will not even be maintained: first, because we have no trained personnel to maintain it; and second, because there's no equipment to maintain it. That adds up to a very short-term life. In that regard, from an economic development point of view, we were fostering additional layers of economic dependence, not economic independence. Any of you who tracked this in Ohio know that the governor made very strong statements about it when he returned.

Let me just stop here and respond to any questions you might have, either on the state's question or on the economic development question.

Q: [speaker from Maryland] Some of us here tonight are from other states. I wonder if you have any recommendations for someone who might want to be a citizen lobbyist here to get the guard out of Honduras?

A: Well, I guess I would say the same thing I would say about a different issue that is just beginning in Ohio: I think you need to know your governor's position, because there is no action for Maryland to take unless the governor is willing to stand up for the states' rights issues involved here. You need to know the policy position of the adjutant general of your state and the policy

69

position of your governor. And then you might put together—and this is something our office could help with—a tracking of what has been done (particularly the Perpich case in Minnesota) and the trail of what has happened here in Ohio. I am sure, like any other grass-roots influence process, if this kind of citizens' lobby popped up in a lot of places in America, the chips would shift: it would be a balance that would shift in terms of the governor's capacity to influence the system versus what at this point is pretty much just a threat. (We were told, for example, "If you don't play ball, we will take this installation out of Ohio and we will put it in Indiana.")

Q: Can you say a little bit about the questionable need for roads? I wonder if you could say anything about whether there is a human need for these roads. Are they going to be a farm-to-market type arrangement?

A: I feel very respectful of my own lack of experience in this particular region, but let me speak specifically about the Yoro Province in Honduras, which is the only one that we saw on site.

As is true in many Latin American countries, the major economic issue, or major dilemma, is unemployment. The pattern that is developing is an extraordinary influx of youth out of villages—and virtually tribal kinds of living situations high in the mountains—into major metropolitan areas where the social services systems are breaking down, where they are unable to create new jobs on an annual basis to absorb that population. So I believe that a true economic development plan in the Yoro Province would be in fact to assist small industries and develop other kinds of agricultural production to create jobs.

Q: These threats: where are they coming from? Are they coming from the White House, and are they legal?

A: Well, they are legal if the Montgomery amendment is upheld, because the essence of the Montgomery amendment now takes precedence over the governor's commander in chief role in the states, *even* in peacetime.

Q: But the threats were being made before the threats.

A: This is true. I wish I could read you the telegram that we received. I am speaking very straight now. Could we have taken some kind of retaliatory action on the basis of how they did this? No. We were dealing with a much more sophisticated bureaucratic process than that. Things like what I said to this gentleman over here—about the statement that the installation be in Indiana instead—were all verbal processes.

Q: And the threats came from where?

A: The National Guard Bureau. Now at this moment I realize I made a choice that is typical of me: to be very candid. Obviously, abuse of the kind of conversation I am having with you would be damaging if it were taken out of context or manipulated to take on a different meaning.

I have been warned that I have got about five minutes. Let me get to the last area I said I would talk about and I have not talked about yet, and that is about Governor Celeste's belief about peace in Central America.

The governor's trip to Honduras took place in July of 1987. I do not remember the dates specifically, but the extraordinary initiative that was taken by President Arias of Costa Rica happened in that late summer-fall period of time. What Governor Celeste tried to do was build on his experience in Honduras and send as strong a message as possible from the Statehouse to the White House: "This is the beginning of a potential peace process in Central America, and it is being done by the leadership of the nations that make up that region."

One of the things that I remember from this trip to Honduras was that the Governor sat with a very high-ranking member of the Honduran government—not the military, but the government. He asked, "What should America's policy be in Central America?" He asked the question about Central America, not just Honduras, and the response that he was given has been quoted many times since then: "America should use its role as a superpower to negotiate directly with the Russians to mutually achieve peace in Central America."

Essentially, the response was, "Play your leadership role where your leadership is. Play your leadership role where *your* president and Congress can take advantage of the changed potential atmosphere in Central America and give *us* an opportunity to follow through on the area's peace proposal." The communication that Governor Celeste sent to President Reagan—and then reiterated to Defense Secretary Carlucci in March, when Operation Golden Pheasant dropped thirty-two hundred people into Central America—was, basically, that it is a changed world with Gorbachev's role in Russia, and with the Reagan-Gorbachev process. We must shift our focus and look at what we can do *respon-*

sively in terms of capitalism and communism stepping back and allowing a different direction to evolve.

Again, I am sure you have heard a great deal this afternoon about how well or how fully the U.S. has or has not played out that role. However, Governor Celeste's consistent message has been that, by definition, the people in Central America should be allowed to evolve in the direction themselves; and, when that direction has some stability, we should reenter as we have done many times around the world with aid that is truly in the spirit of development, which empowers people, and enables them to set up the link to eventual economic independence.

That is the vision that the governor would like to see played out.

6

THE PROBLEMS OF PEACE IN CENTRAL AMERICA:
A LATIN AMERICAN PERSPECTIVE

Manuel Rodríguez Arriaga

Diversity and Change

In 1963, President John F. Kennedy said about Latin America, "If we do not end our differences now, at least we can create a world safe for diversity." A quarter century has passed since then. Diversity persists but our world is in no way safer, not for Latin America, not for the relations between it and the United States. It is not safer because the diversity of our continent has not been understood nor accepted, because its diversity has been seen as a problem and not as a product of history that it is necessary to respect in order to have a safer world.

As the decade ends, it is the Central American conflict that sums up our world of diversity, change, and contradiction. It was a decade of cold war, of regional conflicts, of ideological anachronisms, of intolerance and renewed hegemony; a decade of economic crisis for most nations, crisis of insufficient production and growth, crisis of debt and development, crisis of the very concept of interdependence—stability in crisis, if you will. Today we face the moral and political imperative of promoting peace in Central America. The reasons for acting quickly and firmly, for Latin America, are many and important.

The conflict continues, causing death, political repression, and economic regression, which means intolerable sacrifice and irreversible harm for the peoples of Central America. The conflict casts doubt on the validity of the international legal order as it witnesses the systematic violation of norms and principles essential to the harmonious coexistence of nations. The conflict affects the legitimate national interests of Latin

American countries. The conflict distorts ties of solidarity and cooperation between the conflicting nations and others of Latin America. The conflict causes damage to the political relations between Latin America and the United States.

Incomprehensions

In Latin America it is frequently said that our differences with United States policy are "due to incomprehension," that is, caused by an erroneous perception of the region's conflict, incomprehension of the nature and origin of the crisis, incomprehension of the reasons for Latin American initiatives.

Writer Carlos Fuentes has summed up with clarity four difficulties for the United States in identifying change in Latin America. The first is difficulty in identifying the cultural context of change. The second is difficulty in identifying nationalism as a historical force for change. The third is difficulty in identifying problems of international redistribution of power in its effects on the countries of the region. The fourth is difficulty in identifying the bases for negotiation of these themes when they become themes of conflict between Latin America and the United States.

In any case, in our opinion, the capacity to understand the times of change in Central America and to recognize the rhythm of its peoples' history continues to be on trial. There is an inability to understand that the origin of its social transformation is not in subversion nor in exporting revolution and that these would be ineffective, even if attempted, if they were not supported by internal conditions. There is lack of understanding that the origin of change in Central America is in the accumulation of contradictions in history: deficiencies, deprivations, and frustrations.

From their own experience of history and of change, Latin Americans understand the crisis that Central America experiences. Having the same history, how could they ignore the deprivations and the aspirations for justice, the struggles to improve living conditions and to participate in the definition of their own political destiny? How could Mexico, for example, ignore them when it was a target for threats, coercion, and two armed interventions because of its own social revolution?

Today it seems absurd, but it did not seem so in 1927 to Calvin Coolidge, when he called on the Congress of the United States to accuse the government of Mexico and its revolution of being the sources of Bolshevik revolution in Central America. Incomprehension, perhaps. Today it is accepted that revolutionary measures in agrarian reform, lay education, natural resources, labor rights—all anathema in 1927— allowed Mexico to transform itself into a modern nation with productive drive and prolonged stability, with a sense of affirmation and pride, a nation conscious of itself and its surroundings. The process was gradual. It had its contradictory movements and shortcomings. It did not all happen at once; neither growth, social peace, nor democracy.

Disagreements

The Central American conflict reflects, *a grosso modo*, three areas of disagreement between the United States and Latin America: disagreements over the objectives of international political action in the crisis; disagreements over the definition of concepts central to the development of this political action; and disagreements over strategies to follow.

Kindly permit me to clarify that the references I will make to Latin American positions—risking oversimplification—will sum up those of the Permanent Mechanism for Consultation and Concerted Political Action, also called the Group of Eight, composed of Argentina, Brazil, Colombia, Mexico, Peru, Panama, Uruguay, and Venezuela. This group has never presumed to speak for all of Latin America and the Caribbean. It is, however, a group with important influence in the region, one that represents, as a whole, about 90 percent of the inhabitants, territory, and economic production of Latin America.

The eight Latin American governments that also make up Contadora and its Support Group agree that a lasting peace in Central America is possible only through recognition of a region characterized by political diversity, through recognition of a pluralistic region in which governments of different natures coexist.

The United States, to the contrary, has not been willing to accept the Nicaraguan government as one of the elements of life in Central America with the right to exist and continue existing. Nor has it favored negotiation with the Salvadoran rebels who are an undeniable factor in the challenge presented to this country's stability and to the search for regional security.

A second area of disagreement has to do with the definition of concepts central to comprehension and management of the crisis that is

75

the origin of the conflicts: the concepts of regional security, the role of democracy, the extent of foreign intervention, and the significance of the principles and norms of international law, among others. The concepts of security that prevail in Latin America and in the United States in relation to the crisis differ widely. This has perceptible implications regarding the political strategy for each, its basis, and its direction.

At the meeting held a year ago in Acapulco, the presidents of the Group of Eight said that "in order to deepen the actions in favor of development with democracy, justice, and independence (in Latin America), it is necessary to affirm the concept that regional security must heed aspects of peace and stability as well as those concerning political, economic, and financial vulnerability." In the case of Latin America, however, it would seem that the politics of power has imposed its logic; military-strategic and ideological considerations have determined the position of the United States.

Latin America, not only Central America, suffers from what could be called a "special regime." While in the United States it is insisted that we are a "strategic region" according to a unilateral definition of the concept of security, in Latin America the perception states that this special regime does not inspire privileged treatment in financial, commercial, and technological relations, nor in other areas of great importance to our countries. It only responds to political, economic, or military considerations of the United States which belong to a framework of global interests or internal politics. Possibly Latin American countries feel they belong to a circle of relative priorities in U.S. policy, but one that does not necessarily reflect the roots of their problems nor the singularity of the solutions required.

Thus, for example, Latin Americans do not share doctrines of national security and zones of influence that are foreign or contrary to their interests, doctrines which are, in large measure, inapplicable. They also do not want an arms race in an area which, for political and economic reasons, would seriously violate their own definition of security. They also do not want a greater foreign military presence, which would introduce false hopes of strategic alliances incompatible with the objects of independence and sovereignty. Finally, no one wants militarism because—as history shows—this brings with it subordination of power structures to the logic of military interests, reduces maneuvering space for civil governments, and weakens democracy as a form of political action and life.

Latin America no longer wants to be on the brink of military escalations, nor of destabilizing actions, nor of violations of individual and social rights, nor of interventions. It aspires to a life safe for all, where political stability is guaranteed by sustained social and economic development with justice, and where democracy is guaranteed only by Latin Americans.

Similarly, in Latin America, geopolitical hypotheses such as the domino theory are openly questioned. They are thought of as hypotheses which dismiss history, cultural foundations, and the political structures of our societies.

The interpretation of the Central American conflict as originating in the East-West confrontation also is questioned. That the regional crisis absorbed ingredients of that confrontation, as time went on, is recognized in Latin America. However, there is agreement that the origin of political and social instability is found not in the East-West confrontation but in the severe deficiencies of the productive structures, in the profound social imbalances, and in the weakness of political institutions. In Central America, poverty and injustice have translated into frustration and demand and these into repression and even greater social frustration, creating a horrendous dead end with no apparent way out. To this dead end of instability and contradiction arrived—as effect and not as cause—guerrilla activity, rebellion, and foreign intervention.

Origins

The crisis became evident as a regional issue only at the beginning of this decade. Yet its roots are deep. With the exception of Costa Rica, one of the characteristic features of Central America since the end of the Second World War was the consolidation of authoritarian regimes. Economically, penetration and development by transnational corporations were favored for thirty years, particularly in the agricultural exports sector. This gave rise to two decades of sustained growth, but also to severe structural deformation and disproportionate economic and political dependence on the United States.

The crisis of the world economic system that struck hard during the seventies produced recession in Central America, increased the trade balance deficit between those countries and the United States, and aggravated the foreign debt problem. Excessive concentration of wealth and the general inability of political and economic structures to satisfy the population's requirements for mobility and well-being generated increasingly more aggressive forms of social conflict. Some of these gave rise to broad armed national movements such as those of Nicaragua and El Salvador. Others took the form of international incidents such as the war between Honduras and El Salvador. At the beginning of the eighties, internal instability increased in Guatemala, and frequent incursions by its military into Mexican territory in pursuit of guerrillas posed the risk of an incident between the two nations.

As in the majority of the conflicts which rend the contemporary world, that of Central America shows the explosive potential of economic and social backwardness. At the same time, it shows the conditioning factors external to ideological pluralism, to self-determination of peoples, to their development, to internal conciliatory efforts, and to regional negotiation. Thus we maintain that development is the best foundation, perhaps the only foundation, for achieving institutional and political stability in Central America. Without a doubt, it is the best proposal for security in the long run that can be made to these countries. On it depends in every case the advancement of democracy.

Here should be mentioned a highly polemicized question and one that has done great damage to the conflict's recent history: use of the so-called "commitment to democracy" to intervene, openly or covertly, in the internal affairs of Central American nations. Support of democracy cannot justify any attack on sovereignty; nor can support for the principle of self-determination be the basis of foreign acts of intervention. Defense of legal and moral values which means the violation of other equally important values deserving respect is inappropriate.

Furthermore, each nation must build, on its own, its democracy, taking inspiration from its social experience, its culture, its collective longings, its concrete reality. No two democracies are alike; there are no absolute, inevitable formulas in this area. In short, there's no room for intervention to establish democracy.

Strategies

A true easing of tensions in the Central American conflict, as in any other regional conflict, can only occur through unconditional subordination of states to the principles and norms of international law. In this sense, negotiation is the natural way to a peaceful solution of controversies. These norms and principles have been fundamental for Latin American activities in regard to the problem of Central America.

The Contadora and its Support Group have insisted that any peace strategy must be based on diplomacy, never on force. For the same reason, they could not have accepted the so-called "two-track policy."

Latin America has suffered a great deal from the effects of foreign intervention and the politics of power in general. From this stems the struggle to make respect for international law one of the top priorities of Latin American democracies. In this there can be no concessions. Sovereignty is at risk. To ignore violations of the law by the powerful would mean opening the way for new violations in the future, possibly to the detriment of our own country's interests and of the legal and political regional security.

The systematic use of force in Central America has weakened the negotiation process; it has fomented violence, reduced the maneuvering capacity of mediating governments, and radicalized positions. Moreover, it has not solved even one of the region's problems. In fact, many have worsened. Economic and social problems are more severe, the precarious advances of democracy are threatened, the militarization of some countries continues, and the dignity and sovereignty of those nations continue to suffer.

Initiatives

In January 1983, the Latin American diplomatic peace initiative for Central America, known as the Contadora Group, brought together Colombia, Mexico, Panama, and Venezuela in concerted action. It began from the evaluation of the risks which the conflict in Nicaragua implied for stability in the area. It also began from the knowledge of the problem's historical roots and the necessity of achieving a peaceful solution based on negotiations and respect for international law and human rights. The group's efforts were guided from the beginning by three interrelated objectives: avoid a conflagration in the area, promote a regional peace agreement, and contribute to the economic and social development of Central America.

Contadora's first task was to set up a process of negotiation among the Central American governments based on the following political criteria: (1) consideration of the legitimate security interests of the nations in conflict, (2) search for a balance between those interests and the requirements of regional security, (3) respect for self-determination of neighboring states by the area's governments, (4) demand for nonintervention by governments outside the region, (5) separation of the crisis from the East-West confrontation, (6) recognition that Central American governments have the untransferable obligation to achieve peace while at the same time preserving the security interests of Latin America.

In relation to the last point, it should be mentioned that the effort of Contadora never has sought to displace commitments or usurp powers, nor to be a regional power that imposes conditions from a position of strength. It has tried, instead, to open a Latin American alternative to the crisis with full knowledge of the facts, with moral authority and just proposals. At the same time, and as the presidents of the Group of Eight have said, "Peace in Central America is a priority of our nations because not only is the consolidation of democracy and development with self-determination of Central American nations at stake, but also the national interests of our countries."

The four Latin American governments understood from the beginning that worsening or extension of the conflict in Nicaragua would inevitably provoke a greater refugee displacement within the area and toward neighboring countries, an even more serious breakdown in the productive structures, and disruption of communications and obstruction of commercial and financial ties in the region. All of this would end up rending the social fabric of Central America with irreversible consequences. The crisis in Central America would escalate to greater levels of political and economic instability in a vicious circle and would imply increasing institutional fragility beyond repair.

After ten months of persistent work beset with enormous obstacles, the Contadora initiative produced the Document of Objectives, the first general political agreement signed by the Central American governments. This agreement stated fundamental commitments for meeting the gravest aspects of the crisis. Starting from realistic diagnosis and from a reaffirmation of basic international legal principles, it identified the security objectives that regional reconciliation efforts would have to pursue. A channel for negotiation was definitely opened. Until then, some Central American governments had refused all dialogues, not accepting any negotiating basis. The initiative continued with the Norms for the Carrying Out of Commitments Assumed in the Document of Objectives. That meant defining approaches and criteria necessary to respond to the crisis's main regional problems, based on concrete agreements.

During 1984, Contadora's actions contributed to slowing down the extension of the conflict. That year the first Supervisory and

Prevention Commission was set up for the purpose of circumventing and reducing border tensions between Costa Rica and Nicaragua. Similar efforts were carried out to prevent border conflicts between Honduras and Nicaragua. Also that year, as a result of the diplomatic work of the Mexican government, representatives of the United States and Nicaraguan governments met in Manzanillo, Mexico. During five different meetings, representatives searched for greater understanding of interests and security problems; they sought reduction of tensions and the eventual normalization of bilateral relations, both proposals for resolving the regional conflict. Nevertheless, in 1985 conversations were suspended.

In May of that year, with negotiations at a relative standstill, Argentina, Brazil, Peru and Uruguay formed the Contadora Support Group, thereby broadening joint Latin American action and demonstrating, without reservations, a strong, unified will for a diplomatic solution to the conflict. At the same time, a precedent was established: to search for Latin American solutions to essentially Latin American problems.

Another encouraging and significant step was the first meeting of Central American, Contadora, and European Foreign Ministers. In San José, Costa Rica, the Europeans ratified unanimously their backing of Contadora's initiatives and, in general, of resolving the regional conflict peacefully rather than by force. Similarly, they promised to support efforts for economic development and integration in the isthmus. Four annual meetings have been held pursuing these same objectives, the most recent in Hamburg last March [1988].

During 1985 and part of 1986, negotiations took place to draw up a broad regional treaty. Under the leadership of Contadora, the governments of Central America drew closer to a series of specific agreements that sought to respond to the different areas of the conflict and create a system of security and cooperation for development.

In 1986, this Latin American effort resulted in meetings attended by more than one hundred government representatives from Costa Rica, El Salvador, Guatemala, Honduras, and Nicaragua. Five negotiating groups worked on identifying elements for a treaty project with four main sections: (1) political commitments, (2) security commitments, (3) economic and social commitments, and (4) mechanisms for carrying out the commitments. The project, called the Contadora Act for Peace and Cooperation in Central America, attempted to secure the promise from various states with ties and interests in the region, especially the United

81

States and Cuba, to support and respect the agreements adopted by the five isthmus nations.

In June of 1986, the final version of the Contadora act was presented to the consideration of all governments of the region. In the opinion of the Latin American governments, the document achieved a just and reasonable balance among the legitimate interests of the various states. It proposed simultaneous attention to the different manifestations of the crisis. Lamentably, some Central American governments decided not to sign the treaty even after they had taken an active part in its negotiation. The reasons for their refusal were never made clear. Publicly, not one valid argument was raised against the treaty, nothing to justify the obstinate but evident resistance to make a commitment to peace. Formally, no one opposed signing nor continuing negotiations. But the obstacles remained and the process came to a virtual standstill. During the following months tensions gradually increased.

That same year, faced with the risks implied by a diplomatic vacuum, the Contadora and its Support Group emphasized in their Declaration of Caraballeda the urgent necessity for Central American governments to freeze arms acquisitions, take concrete measures for national reconciliation, and guarantee human rights. The group proposed, the urgency of ending external support to irregular forces and rebel movements which had operated in the area.

A new attempt to reactivate peace negotiations occurred at the beginning of 1987 when, in an unusual diplomatic action, the foreign ministers of the Contadora and the Support Group visited the five Central American capitals with the secretaries-general of the United Nations and the Organization of American States. As a result of interviews with chiefs of state and other high officials of those countries, measures were proposed to provide a basis of trust among the conflicting parties to permit serious negotiations. Nevertheless, lack of political will made the movement toward peace remain at a standstill.

Despite failures and frustrations, the Latin American initiative formed the basis for the Esquipulas Agreement, signed by the five Central American presidents in August 1987. The peace proposal of the president of Costa Rica, which had given rise to the agreement, was composed in essence of elements of the Contadora act. In Esquipulas, the Central American governments promised to renew negotiations and fulfill certain fundamental obligations in the areas of regional security and national reconciliation. In this context, they proposed participation of the eight Latin American ministers in the International Verification

82

Commission, made up also by Central Americans and representatives of UN and OAS Secretaries-General, in supervising the fulfillment of the Esquipulas commitments.

A few months later, in January 1987, the commission disintegrated. The conclusions resulting from its first efforts met with disapproval from various governments of the region. By pointing out the nonobservance of Esquipulas and by noting increased human rights violations in various countries, the commission dug its own grave. Its report also made it clear that some governments had their own and differing interpretations of the obligations assumed; de facto, the agreement of the Central American presidents was in question. It likewise showed that peace in the region would remain distant while governments from outside the area continued intervening and blocking the negotiation process and the observance of the agreements.

Since then, on various occasions the five Central American governments have expressed their wish that the eight Latin American states make new contributions to negotiations, that they once again exercise their good offices. However, in practice, grounds for new initiatives are lacking. The standstill will continue.

In spite of lack of new initiatives, Contadora's push toward international cooperation for economic and social development in Central America is advancing. The Energy Cooperation Program for Central America and the Caribbean, established by Mexico and Venezuela in 1983, known as the San José Pact, has been renewed yearly. It continues to guarantee a supply of hydrocarbons to nine countries on a preferential basis, thus supporting the objective of contributing to the region's stability.

My Mexican initiative in 1984, the Committee for Support of Economic and Social Development of Central America (CADESCA), was established within the framework of the Latin American Economic System (SELA). Faced with the destruction of the region's economies and inspired by a spirit of solidarity, twenty-one countries of the region joined the effort. The committee's task is to collect resources from countries that wish to support Central American development.

In their summit meeting in Acapulco, the heads of state of the Group of Eight agreed to promote an international emergency economic reconstruction plan for Central America. They proposed plans for stimulating interregional trade, granting facilities for Central American exports, obtaining resources for the region's financial institutions, and backing subregional integration and specific projects in priority areas

83

such as agricultural production and human resources training. That initiative contributed to the formation of the Special Plan for Economic Cooperation in Central America in May of this year [1988], approved by the General Assembly of the UN and coordinated by the United Nations Development Program (UNDP).

Finally, the strengthening of bilateral cooperation between the Contadora and Support Group countries and those of Central America should be mentioned. The most ambitious program was initiated by Mexico, also in May, under the name of Cooperation Plan for Central America. Via systematic and planned action, it seeks to foment economic, technical, scientific, and cultural relations with nations of the region, based on respect and fairness. Mexico understands that to contribute to the development of such nations is to meet its commitment to solidarity and, at the same time, to foster regional security and harmony favorable to its own development.

The proposals of Contadora continue being essentially valid. Their activity, beginning in 1983, allowed a space to be opened for negotiation and thus avoided a solution by force. Belligerent actions that seemed to presage a regional war never got out of hand. If there had been war, consequences for Central Americans, for all of Latin Americans, and for relations with the United States, would have been disastrous.

International consciousness concerning the crisis—its causes and implications—has extended gradually, putting new obstacles in the path of the politics of force. Within Central American countries, voices of tolerance have grown favorably disposed toward reconciliation and negotiations and prepared for an honest commitment to democracy and self-determination.

International cooperation to support economic and social development of the region's nations has also grown with considerable promise. Contadora's initiatives have received broad support from international and regional organizations, as well as from governments, parliaments, and political parties of numerous nations. If the governments of Canada, Western and Eastern Europe, and of the nonaligned countries, among others, sided with the Latin American efforts for peace, it was because of the rightness of those efforts, because of the negative implications of the use of force in the region, and because a war would have deteriorated international conditions dramatically.

The current standstill in negotiations, however, has potential dangers which must be avoided. Esquipulas could suffer an irreversible freeze-out due to nonobservance of its terms. This could produce isolation of the situation, or, of one of the countries in conflict isolation in order to impose imbalanced agreements. Likewise, this could increase the presence of extraregional interests in the case of withdrawal of Latin American mediation. Solutions through force could find a suitable climate and provoke a worsening of belligerent actions.

Opportunities

Latin America nations have been linked by history, culture, and language. Today, in addition, they are linked by the extension of democracy, a sense of constructive independence, a call to development, and the common challenge of a deep economic crisis. These all encourage feelings of solidarity and increased capacity for concerted action.

It is not an exaggeration to affirm that the Central American crisis continues to test relations between Latin America and the United States. The resolution of the regional conflict or its indefinite prolongation could condition a significant part of the relationship between the Americas in the future. For Latin America, the conflict must be resolved by negotiation, one which recognizes Central America's diversity and one which builds up forms of coexistence on the foundations of that diversity and the times dictated by its own history.

For Latin America, force is not an option and it has not been during the decade of the 1980s. The complexity of the conflict demands much more: reconciliation, not imposition; tolerance, not dogma; investment in development rather than in destructive arms. For their problems, Latin Americans want peaceful solutions, solutions forged by them. They are prepared to propose, to mediate, and to act. They want no more Central American crises.

In any case, Central America will no longer be what it was. Despite political repression and deterioration, intervention and economic regression, the process of mediation for peace opened consciousness and language. It opened opportunities for national reconciliation and international understanding about the need for change.

We believe the United States of America also will not stay the same. It cannot, because it will find that Central America and, in general, Latin America, are changing irreversibly. It cannot, because in its domestic politics there has also been some kind of change. Today the Central American crisis and everything else about Latin America are widely debated, written about, and questioned. Political instability, economic crisis, expanding democracy, and strengthened diplomatic action have become themes of significant analysis and inquiry within American political society.

There is in the United States a growing consciousness about the contradictions and deficiencies that the regional conflict expresses, as well as about Latin American vision and initiative. The debate has contributed to the improvement of the flow of information and the reinforcement of attempts at solution. In this context, there is a double challenge for the ties between the United States and Latin American countries that is encouraging to us. One is of will and the other is of imagination: will to reconcile perceptions, interests, and actions in relation to superior objectives, peace and development in Central America; and imagination to define new, realistic, and viable ways towards a reasonable solution.

Central America ought to be on the agenda for renewed dialogue between Latin America and the United States that responds to times of change and diversity and enriches, not damages, our complex and inevitable relationship. A week ago [22 October 1988] in Punta del Este, the heads of state of Argentina, Brazil, Colombia, Mexico, Peru, Uruguay, and Venezuela declared the following in a joint statement:

> Relations between Latin America and the United States are at a challenging stage that demands renewed political capacity and a strong will to understanding. Differences in interests and perceptions have not permitted fully taking advantage of opportunities for broader and more equal cooperation. It is necessary, therefore, to encourage a climate of trust and understanding. For this, we propose immediate dialogue on the political, economic, and social problems that affect us.

Days before, the president of Mexico, Miguel de la Madrid, had proposed "a special reflection on the relations between Latin America and the United States; on the importance of building a new phase of communication, of cooperation and negotiation in favor of new generations; on a way of reducing, for that end, antagonism and distrust."

The president also said,

We want to think that the moment is right; that we can significantly diminish differences in interests and political perception; that we are capable, both north and south of the continent, of understanding the changes our respective societies are experiencing; and that we can foresee, with opportunity and realism, those changes which will define tomorrow. . . . We are better prepared to act in a world more diverse and more competitive. We are also better prepared to reach an understanding with the United States that is truly fair, forged in mutual respect, nurtured by the objective of generating progress and distributing its benefits with a sense of justice and stability.

Ladies and gentlemen, we shall contribute, with the common reflection that this meeting at Ohio University provides, to those fair objectives. We shall contribute with our action—as modest as it may seem—to deepening the channels of understanding. We, all of us, deserve better times, times of security, cooperation, and certainty. First and foremost, the people of Central America deserve it; they are people who want to be protagonists in their own times of development, of self-determination, of peace.

NICARAGUA: CONTINUING MYTHS, ONGOING REALITIES

Robert M. Witajewski

A fundamental, continuing goal of United States policy in Central America has been to encourage democratic and economic development within the context of Latin American history and culture.* Decision makers of President Ronald Reagan's administration have been well aware of, and sensitive to, the historical context within which U.S. policy in Central America must operate, the fundamental principles of international relations, and the realities of bureaucratic politics so succinctly characterized by Graham T. Allison, the well-known author of *Essence of Decision* [Boston: Little, Brown, 1971].

United States policy toward Nicaragua must be viewed as the result of this intersection of forces. U.S. policy, and the motivations behind it, are the result of a complex, ongoing process reflecting domestic, political, and bureaucratic considerations, U.S.-Soviet relations, broader forces of international relations, and the actions of the Sandinista National Liberation Front (FSLN) leaders. Sandinista leaders, therefore, should not delude themselves by believing that they merited the intense and ongoing interest of the Reagan administration during the decade of the 1980s. Similarly, the student of international relations would do well to avoid the analytical error of seeking a unitary explanation of United States-Nicaraguan relations outside of the broader context of bipolar and multilateral events involving the United States.

---

*While the original presentation was made in late 1988, the material in this chapter has been revised and updated to reflect information and statistics available through August 1989.

That Nicaragua became a key focal point for the policy makers of the Reagan administration, with the consequences which this had for Nicaragua's society and economy in the last ten years, flows essentially from deliberate decisions by the Sandinista leadership to attempt to secure and consolidate their overthrow of the dictator Anastasio Somoza Debayle through export and expansion and the requirement of the United States to react to this decision.

Sandinista leaders, aided and abetted by Cuban and Soviet advisors and mentors, decided not to focus on creating a self-contained revolution "in one country." In June 1981, President Daniel Ortega announced that the principles of Marxism-Leninism would serve as the guide of the Nicaraguan revolution. Sandinista leaders periodically repeated this refrain. In January 1989, for example, while preparing for the Sandinista's tenth anniversary in power, Commandant Victor Tirado, a member of the FSLN directorate and chief of labor activities for the Sandinista mass organizations, proclaimed that "Sandinismo is a doctrine of modern revolutionary thought in Latin America," and, therefore, must extend far beyond Nicaragua's borders. The support of the Soviet Union and its Cuban surrogate in this gambit could not go unchallenged by the United States.

Myth 1. Nicaragua, a small country, is not a threat to anyone and, thus, the United States can ignore events occurring there.

A key element of the Sandinista game plan was to screen off and divert international attention from the Soviet Union's crucial role in providing the Sandinista leadership with the resources needed to carry out their program for most of the decade of the 1980s. To the extent that the Sandinistas could portray the issue not as one of the world's two superpowers playing a gambit in the security zone of the other, but rather as that of a tiny, insignificant Third World country seeking only to maintain its autonomy and sovereignty against the "Colossus of the North," they would be able to significantly increase the odds of successfully carrying out their game plan. This myth, although expertly packaged and promoted, never corresponded to the reality during the decade of the 1980s.

In one sense—the crudest and most irrelevant—the myth is true. Nicaragua does not present a direct military threat to the United States. This is a true statement, but one that to the student of international relations is both simplistic and irrelevant. Of more immediate relevance is that Nicaragua, acting in the real world with the backing of the Soviet Union, does present a security threat to both its immediate regional neighbors and to U.S. regional interests.

Expanding from the relatively small size of the Guardia Nacional as it existed under the Somozas, by 1988 the Sandinista armed forces had increased in size to about 80,000 persons with direct subsidization from the Soviet bloc (Table 1). Soviet bloc arms shipments to Nicaragua alone for the period 1982-1987 exceeded U.S. security assistance to the entire region for the same period. By 1989, the Sandinista leadership had increased the size of the Nicaraguan armed forces to a total of over 180,000 persons, including regular military, reserves, militia, and internal security forces. In contrast, the combined military forces of the four Central American democracies during this same period was under 132,000. In this context, a Nicaraguan armed force of 80,000 far exceeds what almost anyone would rationally conclude was a legitimate national security need.

Table 1

SIZE OF REGULAR ARMY IN CENTRAL
AMERICAN COUNTRIES (1988)

Country	Size
Nicaragua	80,000
El Salvador	43,600
Honduras	17,250
Guatemala	36,000
Costa Rica	0

Soviet bloc military shipments to Nicaragua through early 1989 have an estimated cumulative value of approximately $2.9 billion (Table 2). In 1989 through mid-May, Soviet bloc arm shipments to Nicaragua were estimated at $175 million (Table 2). Since 1986, annual Soviet bloc arms shipments to Nicaragua have exceeded an estimated $500 million and, despite an absence of formal hostilities, show no sign of decreasing. Since signing the Sapoá agreement with resistance in March 1988, the Sandanistas have received over $585 million in military aid.

Eight armed transport helicopters (model MI-17) were delivered in November 1988. Through mid-1989, Nicaraguan military imports from Cuba and Soviet bloc countries continued. In 1989, these shipments included three North Korean Sinhung patrol boats.

Table 2

SOVIET BLOC MILITARY ASSISTANCE TO NICARAGUA
1980-1989 (in 000 tons and millions of dollars)

Year	Arms Shipments (tons)	Metric Tons	Estimated Value (dollars)
1980	--	1.6	$ 10
1981	2	9.5	160
1982	6	11.2	140
1983	25	13.9	250
1984	37	20.0	370
1985	35	19.4	250
1986	50	22.0	550
1987	60	22.0	500
1988	68	19.0	515
1989	29	7.4	175

Nicaraguan's Central American neighbors have the legitimate right to ask if a military force of this size is intended for defensive purposes, or whether it has an ulterior motive. Given the security dilemma facing a head of state, the head of state of Honduras or El Salvador could reasonably conclude that the purpose of the massive Sandinista armed forces, combined with expansionist Sandinista rhetoric, was intimidation and aggrandizement, rather than self-defense.

The Sandinista leadership has actively promoted and encouraged instability and violence in the region. According to President Ortega, armed struggle is the best and most secure manner for gaining power. In February 1989 he declared that violence was the best way to gain and maintain power. The FSLN continues active support of terrorist groups in Honduras and Guatemala.

Not only are there links between the M-19 guerrillas in Colombia, but President Daniel Ortega himself has admitted that the FSLN has supported the Farabundo Martí National Liberation Front (FMLN) guerrillas in Salvador. The Sandinista leadership believes that its philosophy and economic principles gave it the right to try to overthrow the democratically chosen government of José Napoleón Duarte in El Salvador and to continue to do so with his democratically selected successor, President Alfredo Cristiani. Public disclaimers to the contrary notwithstanding, this support continues to the present day. On 30 May 1989, the Salvadoran police discovered a cache of 300 Soviet bloc-manufactured AK-47s, 300,000 rounds of ammunition manufactured in Cuba, and 1,000 pounds of explosives. These items are believed to have been transshipped through Cuba and Nicaragua.

The FMLN headquarters in Nicaragua remains the central command and control entity. Guerrilla troops and commanders routinely travel to Nicaragua for training, meetings, and strategy sessions. An estimated 70 percent of the FMLN's ammunition needs come from Nicaragua and Cuba. Information from defectors and other intelligence clearly shows Nicaraguan involvement in providing vessels to transport material from Nicaragua to offshore points where cargo is transferred to smaller boats for delivery to the FMLN inside El Salvador.

This issue of supplying military equipment is critical because the Sandinistas have blatantly disregarded the sacred Latin American principle of nonintervention which they so frequently invoke in their own defense. Apparently, to paraphrase a famous European statesman, to the Sandinistas "intervention" is a philosophical term which means exactly the same as "nonintervention," depending which better suits their needs of the moment. The problem for the U.S. policy maker is that this philosophical laissez faire is occurring in a critical region of the world.

Central America is a region facing serious demographic and economic problems. Populations are from 38 percent to almost 59 percent urban. Annual growth rates vary from 1.2 percent in El Salvador to 3.6 percent in Honduras (Table 3). It is a region which should be devoting its resources to economic development rather than being forced to divert its scarce resources to the immediate needs of self-defense. It is a region that has high unemployment and a very young population, both of which have generated a desperate need for

92

schools, factories, hospitals, roads, and trunk lines. Access to roads is vital for small farmers and peasants so that they can get their products to market and get a better price for them instead of having to sell them at a low price in the nearest village.

As a region, Mexico, the Caribbean, and Central America are the largest sources of illegal immigration in the U.S. Most of this vast population movement is motivated by a search for economic opportunity. If with its limited resources the U.S. is able to assist these countries in reaching self-sustaining growth, then it would reduce the incentive to migrate to the United States in search of jobs. As a result, individuals would be able to stay with their families.

Table 3

CENTRAL AMERICAN POPULATION
CHARACTERISTICS (1987)

Country	Population	Percent Urban	Annual Growth Rate (percent)
Costa Rica	2,791	49.6	2.9
El Salvador	4,934	47.7	1.2
Guatemala	8,434	38.2	2.9
Honduras	4,679	41.4	3.6
Nicaragua	3,501	58.7	3.4

(Source: *Economic and Social Progress in Latin America*, 1988 Report.)

Instability makes popular government extremely difficult. The democratically elected governments of Vinicio Cerezo, Napoleón Duarte, Jose Azcona, and Oscar Arias, like most governments in the world, have only a limited amount in financial resources at their disposal. They *can* use them to build up their infrastructure. When faced with a clear and immediate threat they *must* use them to defend themselves. This requirement to focus on immediate survival and to defer long-term societal needs creates a cycle of instability which feeds upon itself. The moderate political leader in Central America faces the particularly unenviable task of satisfying conservative elements who focus most exclusively on the immediate security threat to the country, social activists who consider the security threat irrelevant and who, instead, focus on longer-term demographic threats, and subversive groups seeking to exacerbate economic and social problems and destabilize the system for their own ends. Unfortunately for Central America this cycle of instability has been a constant on the political landscape for decades, effectively diverting economic and political resources from focusing on how to provide a better life for the people.

The countries of Central America desperately need economic assistance. While the United States has been generous in its development assistance, in a country such as El Salvador its impact has been negated because an insurgent movement has destroyed the equivalent of U.S. aid in a deliberate, concerted, callous attack upon the country's economic infrastructure. Nicaragua's role in the cycle of instability is critical and explains why the United States could not let go unchallenged the Sandinistas' plans to exploit and exacerbate the region's instability for its own ends by providing psychological and material support for groups more interested in destroying systems than changing them, tearing down structures rather than building better ones.

Myth 2. The Sandinista leadership is engaged in a noble economic experiment whose sole purpose is to better their population's living conditions.

For many people, a short drive in from Managua's Sandino International Airport to what used to be Managua's city center will be sufficient to disabuse them of the truth of the following story on Nicaragua's economic situation. In the story a poor peasant, rummaging through one of the city's dumps trying to find something edible to eat, is quoted as saying that "the only thing the revolution has done for us is make us happy."

Even within the communist camp Sandinista economic incompetence must be record setting. So bad is the Sandinistas' economic record that even the Soviet Union will not acknowledge that the Nicaraguans are a part of the socialist camp. Nicaragua's inflation rate in 1988 was somewhere between the 18,000 percent measured by the U.S. Embassy (in a monthly survey measuring the cost of a typical market basket of goods for a low- and middle-income family living in Managua) and the 33,000 percent admitted by the Sandinistas. Income for the average Nicaraguan is less than one-half of what is was in 1977.

The standard of living declined over two-thirds in just the last five months of 1988. In 1989, a Sandinista-commissioned study concluded that living standards in Nicaragua had regressed to World War II levels. In 1987, according to official government statistics, the average official wage provided 32 percent of the basic necessities of the population. By January of 1988 this had declined to 24 percent of the basic necessities needed by a typical Nicaraguan family. By January of 1989 this had probably declined further. Gross Domestic Product doubled between 1960 and 1987. Gross Per Capita Product, however, was more in 1960 than in 1987 (Table 4).

As a result of Sandinista economic programs, Nicaragua has become a society in which the people know the value of everything and the price of nothing. Price controls and government subsidies seriously distort and disrupt economic activity. Businessmen now have no way rationally to price products. Some manufacturers have found it makes more economic sense to let their products sit in warehouses, literally melting in the hot tropical sun, than sell them at less than the cost of production. In recent years farmers have been forced to sell crops at less than production costs; ranchers have been forced to sell, or give away, young livestock because it would cost them more to feed it to maturity than they could receive selling it at government-mandated prices, prices which lead to government-mandated bankruptcy.

Table 4

GROSS DOMESTIC AND PER CAPITA PRODUCT
1960-1987

Year	Gross Domestic (millions of dollars)	Per Capita (dollars)
1960	1,461	979
1970	2,849	1,388
1980	2,950	1,065
1987	3,079	878

The government has gone through a series of economic maneuvers and multiple devaluations aimed at stemming this hyperinflation (Table 5). Their regular calls for "cooperation" with the private sector ring hollow when the call for cooperation is almost immediately followed up with a threat or an expropriation. On 13 July 1988, following such a periodic call for cooperation and pledges of having abandoned old, doctrinaire policies, the Sandinistas proceeded to expropriate what was then the largest remaining private business, the San Antonio sugar refinery. Almost a year later, the Sandinista leadership again proclaimed a new era of "good feelings" with the private sector. And again it proceeded to confiscate. On 21 June 1989, the property of three of the country's largest coffee growers was seized following these owners' criticism of government economic policies.

Table 5

INFLATION RATES IN NICARAGUA
1980-1988

Year	Rate (percent)	Year	Rate (percent)
1980	35	1985	334
1981	24	1986	748
1982	25	1987	1,800
1983	33	1988	18,000
1984	50		

The Sandinista leadership claims that it is seeking a new mixed economy which gives a major role to the private entrepreneur. To buttress their arguments that they are creating a mixed economy, they cite figures such as only 12 percent of the available agricultural land is attached to state farms, or that one-third or fewer of the nation's industrial companies are directly administered by the state. What these statistics do not show, however, is the extent to which the FSLN dominates economic activity through a pervasive (and inefficient) system of regulations and controls. In general, the Sandinistas have sought to determine consumer and producer prices, the distribution of raw materials, the level of salaries, and even production rates. The Sandinista goal over the years has been to make the state the sole exporter, importer, and source of foreign exchange. Private companies and farmers have been required to sell their products not only at prices set by the state but also to individuals or organizations selected by the state. In 1978 exports amounted to $567 million dollars, compared to only $240 million dollars in 1988. Private consumption also showed a decrease, from 5,972 million cordobas in 1979 to 2,897 million cordobas in 1986.

The list of Sandinista-induced economic problems is both lengthy and gruesome. A Sandinista-sponsored study has found that per capita output has fallen one-fourth since 1980; and the average living standard has declined 60 percent in the same period. Nicaragua's per capita income by mid-1989 was lower than Haiti's, according to the Sandinista-sponsored study. The Sandinista constitution proclaims, on paper, the right of all workers to strike for living wages. Yet the reality is a 13 November 1988, statement by Agrarian Reform Minister Jaime Wheelock telling sugar workers, "The revolution rewards, but it also punishes. If anyone raises a strike banner here, we will cut off his hands."

The trade deficit is twice that of export earning, yet the government has carefully moved to maintain the loyalty of its core support groups. For some time rather than distributing relief assistance which has been provided by some European and other countries on a non-political basis, the Sandinista government has been providing it on a priority basis, first to some 73,000 government employees, an approximately equal number of defense ministry employees, and about 15,000 interior ministry functionaries, security and regular police forces.

Myth 3. Nicaragua has not cynically manipulated the Central American peace process.

Students of the diplomatic process in Central America are familiar with the basic documents including the Esquipulas accord, the San José declaration, and the Sapoá agreement. In the Esquipulas II accords, the Sandinistas promised to move toward "an authentic democratic process, both pluralistic and participatory," and provide the opposition with broad access to the media. On 22 January 1988, Commandant Bayardo Arce told a cheering crowd of FSLN supporters that if the opposition parties did not return to their holes, "we will crush them."

Many of the prisoners who have been released are now coming forward with reports of torture and widespread violation of their human rights by their Sandinista jailers.   Sandinistas began executions of prisoners and members of Guardia who had surrendered almost immediately after their takeover of power.   One recently released prisoner has reported that beginning 24 July 1979, guards would arrive at Tipitapa prison with lists of names of people who were then taken from cells and shot in an adjacent field.   Twenty-one Honduran citizens who were released have testified that in 1979-1980 hundreds of their fellow prisoners were executed, often on a random basis.   On some occasions, guards reportedly threw hand grenades into cells.   Others were executed for minor infractions of prison regulations.

Sandinista torture methods included the use of hot cells, keeping prisoners in total darkness, subjecting naked prisoners to extremes of heat and cold for days, locking prisoners in morgue-like drawers, subjecting them to electric shock applied to their genitals and using forms of water torture.   Prisoners were fed starvation rations of food.

Americas Watch in August 1988 presented detailed evidence of "a pattern of summary executions committed by government forces against suspected Contra collaborators." In April 1989 *Americas Watch* found that a "recent investigation . . . has found such executions to have continued. . . ."

On 23 March 1988, at Sapoá, the Sandinista government agreed to decree an amnesty for prisoners, to guarantee "unrestricted freedom of expression, as contemplated in the Esquipulas II Accord," to guarantee the right of all political and other exiles to return to Nicaragua without punishment, and to ensure free participation in municipal, national, and Central American parliamentary elections. The San José declaration which was issued at the end of a summit meeting of the Central American countries also calls for democratization, total press freedom, and pluralism.   At Sapoá the government of Nicaragua unconditionally agreed to provide unrestricted freedom of expression.

Contrast this record of agreeing to institute laudable and commendable democratic procedures with the Sandinistas' record of implementation.   The reality is that over the years since 1979, *La Prensa* has been closed repeatedly; nongovernment radio stations have been taken off the air; and independent, nongovernment newscasts have been censored or silenced.

For months, while the government periodically announced an extension of the cease-fire with the Nicaraguan resistance, it continued to engage in a silent offensive in northern Nicaragua. Using a combination of regular military and interior ministry troops, the goal of these operations was to conduct sweeps throughout the countryside, attack resistance units, engage in mass population roundups, and attempt to identify and intimidate anyone suspected of not supporting the Sandinista regime.

Communication students in the United States may have occasional problems with their editors in having their stories published. Their problems pale in comparison to those facing the nongovernment reporter in Nicaragua. In March 1988 when the director of a non-government news program assigned reporters to broadcast news of a strike of a confederation including communist trade unions to protest the government's failure to keep its economic commitments, Minister of the Interior Tomas Borge called Mr. Jose Castillo of Radio Corporacion into his office, told his guards to leave, and proceeded to assault Mr. Castillo. Along with more subtle forms, such overt censorship and intimidation have been regular facts of life in Nicaragua under the Sandinistas.

There are innumerable other examples that the Sandinista pledge to maintain a democratic and pluralistic society in Nicaragua needs to be carefully monitored. The government has also engaged in a vitriolic campaign against Mothers of Political Prisoners, a group of women whose only purpose is to free relatives—sons, cousins, and husbands—who are being held in prison for political reasons. The Sandinistas also have launched repeated attacks upon the cardinal of Nicaragua, Miguel Obando y Bravo, and moved to suppress violently the peaceful protest of some three thousand demonstrators in Nandaime on 10 July 1988, arresting some forty people. The media law in Nicaragua until recently prohibited broadcasting or printing news concerning the economy or the forced draft which did not please the government, as well as stories which were not put in the proper revolutionary perspective or which defamed the leaders of the country.

The operation of the Nicaraguan system of censorship generally has been carried out with some subtlety. In Nicaragua censorship is generally imposed with a telephone call from the Interior Ministry advising you that you have been ordered to cease broadcasting or publishing because of violation of the press law. You probably will not be advised of the specific action which caused the government to act. If you decide to appeal the order, the appeal is heard by Interior Minister Tomas Borge. Lenin Cerna, the head of state security (the DGSE) and the vice-minister of the interior, on 9 January 1989 declared that "security is subordinate to the political project of the Revolution."

Borge himself has publicly characterized his role as "a policeman and I pursue criminals and counterrevolutionaries. . . . The Nicaraguan Interior Ministry is a ministry of a revolutionary country." As might be suspected, there is a very high conviction rate in Nicaragua, and an extremely low rate of reversal on appeal.

Radio Católica was once ordered shut down for broadcasting a sermon by Miguel Cardinal Obando y Bravo. In the same vein, Commandant Doris Tijerino, head of the Sandinista police, on 20 July 1988, summoned Monsignor Osvaldo Mondragon to police headquarters to warn him about an "inflammatory speech" which he had supposedly made the day before. In fact, the speech had been a sermon on brotherly love which the priest had preached to an audience which included, among others, Mother Theresa of Calcutta.

The draft has been a particularly unpopular policy of the government. For the years that it was in effect it resembled the press gangs of eighteenth century England. Government forces would surround movie theaters, baseball stadiums, and simply seize males leaving the theaters or stadiums and ship them off to military camps. Children as young as twelve and thirteen years old have been rounded up and sent off to the military.

The government has made frequent use of a law going back to the Somoza era which allows people to be sentenced administratively for up to six months in prison. For those who believe that the wheels of justice move too slowly in the United States, Nicaragua is a law and order paradise. The public safety law allows the police to remove malcontents quickly and efficiently. The procedure is simple: one policeman arrests you for violation of the law, a second policeman brings charges against you, and the local police chief decides your guilt or innocence. The process is fast, efficient, and effective.

Myth 4. U.S. policy toward Nicaragua is essentially negative.

Over the years the goal of United States policy in Nicaragua has been to seek to promote democracy and to help bring about the same conditions which the Sandinista leadership themselves proclaim are their goals.

In their 12 July 1979 letter to the OAS, the Sandinista junta promised "to let justice prevail . . . and to do so within the legal framework and without revenge or indiscriminate reprisals." In the Esquipulas accord, signed 7 August 1987 in Guatemala City by the five

100

Central American presidents, President Daniel Ortega committed his government to popular participation by the region's citizens in an authentically democratic process. The five presidents pledged themselves to "promote an authentic democratic, pluralistic, and participatory process that includes the promotion of social justice, respect of human rights. . . ."

The accord specifically notes that political parties would have the right to organize, to participate in decision making, and to have access to the media to make their views known. The signers, however, go beyond pledging themselves not to institute restraints on freedom of expression, such as prior censorship, to making a positive commitment. Political groups are guaranteed "broad access to communication media, full exercise of the rights of association and the right to manifest publicly the exercise of their right to free speech, be it oral, written, or televised, as well as freedom of movement by members of political parties in order to proselytize." The five Central American presidents meeting in San José, Costa Rica on 16 January 1988 reaffirmed their commitment to fulfill unconditionally their obligations under the Esquipulas accord including "above all, democratization, which shall include the lifting of the state of emergency, total freedom of the press, political pluralism, and the termination of the use of special courts."

United States goals toward Nicaragua have been consistent with the principles enunciated in Esquipulas and succeeding documents. In 1981, Assistant Secretary of State for Inter-American Affairs Thomas Enders advised the Sandinista leadership that bilateral relations would improve when the Sandinistas ceased interfering in and supporting the guerilla movement seeking to overthrow neighboring El Salvador's government, ceased their arms buildup, and kept their pledges to political and economic pluralism. In 1984 Assistant Secretary of State Langhorne A. Motley proclaimed that "it is U.S. Government policy to support democracy and democratic institutions. This approach is neither interventionist nor a mindless export of ideology." During his visit to four Central American countries in June 1988, Secretary of State George Shultz singled out U.S. objectives for the region as "freedom, economic progress, and peace." Political progress, he continued, "must rest on the foundation of democracy. The basic freedoms that individuals deserve must be relentlessly pursued." During his confirmation hearing before the Senate Foreign Relations Committee on 17 January 1989, Secretary of State James A. Baker III called for a reaffirmation of bipartisan U.S. policy toward Nicaragua grounded on the goals of "democratization, development, and security for every state in the region."

Finally, on 19 July 1989, President Bush reiterated U.S. support for the encouragement of authentic democracy in Nicaragua. In his statement, President Bush noted that "the United States wanted to do its part for the success of the turn toward democracy. We had contributed to the overthrow of Somoza by cutting off military assistance. . . . We provided $118 million in economic and humanitarian assistance to the new Nicaragua government." Turning to the future, President Bush again challenged the Sandinistas to carry out their pledges.

> The Bipartisan Accord with Congress offers an opportunity for better relations between our two countries. We want to see democracy and national reconciliation work in Nicaragua. We remain willing to respond positively if the Sandinistas fulfill their promises—made to the OAS over ten years ago, at Esquipulas, and again last February in El Salvador—to allow Nicaraguans to exercise their democratic rights.

Conclusion

Support for democracy, support for self-determination, support for self-sustaining economic development, and opposition to Soviet and Cuban intervention in hemispheric affairs were fundamental U.S. foreign policy goals ten years ago, and they remain so today. The administration has always believed, and continues to believe, that democratization is the key to the entire peace process in Central America. These remain the fundamental goals for the United States.

In 1979 the United States was prepared to respect the freely expressed will of the Nicaraguan people. In 1989, the United States pledge remains open-ended and unchanged. The citizens of every country should be able to chose their government in free, fair, and honest elections. The United States will respect these decisions. Our hope is that the Sandinistas sincerely share this same commitment.

8

THE SANDINISTA PERSPECTIVE
ON CENTRAL AMERICA

Alejandro Bendaña

I want to thank Mr. Witajewski [the former speaker]. He promised at the beginning of his speech that he was going to talk to us about some myths surrounding Nicaragua. I think he succeeded admirably. I also want to congratulate Ohio University for the debate that is taking place today: an open academic debate involving all of you, unlike partisan speeches often heard in Washington. We have thus been able to hear some notions that might seem outrageous to Washington and extraneous to what it considers to be the Central American agenda. There were references to history; there were references to legality; and there were references to morality. These references were very refreshing to hear and gives us in Nicaragua a lot of hope for a new course in U.S.-Nicaraguan relations. As long as hope is present in people, and we find it present in the American people, we are going to try to overcome this eight-year-long nightmare.

I also think that there is a third aspect worth noting. Today a debate is taking place between the American government and my own, and I guess the fact that we are talking—albeit indirectly—is something to be congratulated, because it's something that has been difficult to achieve. We believe that through discussion and negotiation—and not by means of a historical, illegal, and immoral policy that takes the lives of human beings—our differences eventually could be resolved.

Just a few days before your own [U.S. presidential] election, I am reminded of a similar moment eight years ago when we read a Republican party platform that called on providing support to the resistance against the "Marxist Sandinista" Nicaragua. Early in 1980

103

there were not even any contras. We thus figured that there was not much of a tradition in American politics for presidents following their platforms once they're elected, so maybe that's a lot of rhetoric. We thought that there were going to be difficulties; that is inevitable. History tells us there has never been a revolution without a counterrevolution, and in the history of Latin America there has never been a counterrevolution without the participation of the CIA. History also tells us that!

In the past the United States has opposed projects of social and national change. Even before there was bolshevism, we had U.S. Marines on our soil. A hundred years ago we had American soldiers fighting against liberalism. In the 1910s, we had American soldiers fighting against the Mexican influence; now, subsequently, it is the communist menace, although, with Gorbachev there, the picture is somewhat confused. In any case, we knew there were going to be difficulties—internal, as well as external—because you just do not expect to go so easily about a process of radical income and land redistribution which redresses the social injustices which were perpetrated during the forty-five-year dictatorship of the atrocious Somoza family. And that is going to get you into trouble. People do not like it when their income or land is getting redistributed. Quite clearly, we are going to face some objections. The old orders or patterns of subservience in a region were being upset by a government, a movement that dared to dream of independence.

In any case, had someone told us eight years ago that we were going to witness a full-fledged mercenary army created, directed, organized, and financed in Costa Rica and in Honduras; that CIA manuals would be published advocating selective assassination; that there was going to be a total embargo; that our ports were going to be mined; that our oil depots were going to be destroyed by CIA commandos; that the United States was to turn its back on a judgment of the World Court; indeed, that the whole constitutional system in this country was going to be shaken on account of an obsessive anti-Nicaraguan policy that would even undermine the process of law and justice here internally, we would have said it probably was not going to happen because a new administration would probably be listening to political experts, and not to astrologers. We were wrong. That platform was actually implemented. That policy was carried out. No number of mistakes on our part, no amount of economic mismanagement (we would love to have seen the so-called private sector manage this economy in the midst of a war), no amount of exuberance, of excessive idealism, of imperfection, could have justified the taking of twenty-six thousand Nicaraguan lives.

Well, it is now eight years later and there is one central fact. Coming out of an eight-year-old Hurricane Ronald, now having been devastated by a Hurricane Joan (and who knows what is ahead), we still want to be optimists because of one central fact: the Reagan administration is leaving, but the Sandinista revolution is staying in place. We have stood up to a pressure—military, economic, political, and diplomatic—under which probably most other governments would have collapsed. So we must have been doing something right. We must have been able to count on the support of a majority of the people. But we have been able and continue to be able to endure the cost of defending our independence and our right to self-determination and of trying to achieve a better life, perhaps no longer for ourselves but for our children. In the name of our children, we are able to make sacrifices. Something else, equally important, is surviving the Reagan administration. Despite the depravity of what we have seen in the last eight years—or maybe on account of it—the biggest surge in Latin American history toward the formation of a collective Latin American will and unity, the result of the newfound ability of Latin Americas to put forth their own analysis, their own solutions, and to act upon them, has resulted in the formation of a Contadora group—as you probably heard yesterday—and the subsequent formation of the support group for Contadora. A growth in the movement of the eight countries and the forging of the Esquipulas peace plans by Central American presidents is something unprecedented in Central American history, in fact, in Latin American history. I suppose maybe we will have to build a monument to Ronald Reagan and to Elliott Abrams somewhere because they were the principal forces behind it.

Can you imagine, amidst this new surge of independence which is vitally linked to the resurgence of Latin American democracy and the process of democratization even in Central America, that Honduras and El Salvador would dare to sign a peace plan on 7 August 1987, one which was strongly opposed by the Reagan administration, which termed it two days later as being, "fatally flawed"? Fatally flawed. Why? Because the plan took account of one simple reality: that the Nicaraguan revolution and the Nicaraguan government were legitimate and had legitimate interests. The Nicaraguan revolution was now part of the permanent political landscape of Central America. It is a simple reality recognized by our neighbors, the same ones that are said to be getting

105

subverted, the same ones who are supposed to be the target of our mean, totalitarian, communist, expansionist aims. They were the ones—nobody forced their hands—to sign, along with Daniel Ortega, a document calling for a new regime of coexistence among the Central Americans, the undertaking of both political and security commitments, and the mechanisms of verifications and dialogues among the Central American countries. All of this was done with the participation not only of the other Latin American countries of Contadora but also of the Europeans to help verify commitments because, of course, nobody was asking anybody to take their word on compliance; therefore independent international verification mechanisms were to be established. That dynamic of negotiation is surviving this administration and gives us hope for a new future, because there is a clear-cut Latin American message going out: a message based on principle, on legality, and on history.

Independent of the fact that many governments are not going to agree with the political philosophy of the FSLN, they nonetheless recognize the right of the Nicaraguan people to self-determination. The documents symbolize our neighbors' vote of confidence in our ability to exercise our independence in a responsible manner, because what you have are responsible documents, be they those of Esquipulas, Contadora, or those signed in Acapulco by the eight presidents. These are not documents of confrontation with the United States. Indeed, you could argue that they are attempts to take into account legitimate American interests. They are there: some of the legitimate American concerns. Probably they had not been explained or defined in such a way by this administration, but they were present and they continue to be present because that is another reality which any peace plan has to contain if it's going to work: it must take account of the United States' interest in the region, United States interests defined legally and legitimately, that is, legitimate security interests. Because if U.S. security interests are defined, as they seem to be today, in terms of the wiping of the Sandinistas off the face of the map, we would have a little bit of trouble with that. So would the majority of the Nicaraguan people and the Central Americans, except in a few fascist circles. The governments of Central America and Latin America would have trouble with that not simply because of principle but because of what their own peoples are saying in their own societies, because they will know that an American intervention against Nicaragua would start off riots from one end of Latin America to the other, and they do not want that either.

The point is that there is a way out. The unthinkable even happened during this dynamic of negotiations. We sat down with the contras in March, and the contras did what we thought they would never do. They actually signed at Sapoá the document that the United States government, at that point, was opposed to: a de facto cease-fire. The United States' influence at that point was not strong enough to stop them from signing, but it has been strong enough to stop them from fully implementing both Esquipulas and Sapoá. Why? Principally because the basic premise of American policy has not changed: Nicaragua must be destroyed; the Nicaraguan government has no place in Central America. As long as that's the premise, of course, there are not going to be any definitive advances in the negotiating process for, again, negotiation implies a recognition of your opponent's basic rights, and where that does not exist, nothing is going to happen.

Yet, there are contras and circles, even within the governments of our neighbors, who are willing now to adapt and go into a scheme of coexistence which we feel is quite workable. We may just be the first revolution in history to give the counterrevolution legal and political space in its country. We think that can happen and it should happen because the price we have paid is much too high. The price that is being paid, on account of American policy toward Nicaragua, by Honduras, Costa Rica, and El Salvador is too high for them too. That is why an instrument such as the Arias peace plan can come forth. That is why five Central American presidents can sign it.

Of course, there are problems; you have probably heard of them characterized as contradictions, lack of consistencies, and the problems of implementation. But there is motion, there is a dynamic, and it has to be supported and sustained. It needs that fundamental impulse from the United States. That is what we hope for in a new administration. Because any new administration is going to have to come to recognize the fact that the old policy has failed with regard to Nicaragua. The big "Gipper" was not able to win one in Central America. He was not able to win one against American public opinion; he might have been the great communicator, but poll after poll showed he was unconvincing with regard to Central America. Maybe the American people were trying to tell him something.

We are not out of the woods yet, for there's something else that is very problematic. Yes, Reagan may be leaving, but he is leaving something behind. They are the terms of debate, parameters of discussion, which are set particularly in Washington. They are problematic because for the Republicans and the Democrats—not necessarily all of them—any notions of international law are extraneous. We have talked to congressmen many a time. We bring up points such as that international law states that "you shall not intervene in the internal affairs of your neighbors," "you shall not resort to force," "you shall resort to peaceful settlement of dispute." They then say, "Oh, sure, sure, but that's irrelevant!"

Well, we want to insist that it is relevant, because we often find ourselves debating not necessarily with avid supporters of the Reagan administration but with others who are concerned only with means, not ends. Our position is very simple: the crime must be stopped. Yes, we must discuss and negotiate. However, the crime that is being committed against the Nicaraguan people must be stopped first. There can be no drawing back from that very conclusion.

Even though we may be discussing with the contras, that does not justify what has been approved recently by both houses and both parties in the U.S. Congress, namely, the contra army is to continue in existence. "God forbid that they should be abandoned! Oh, well, maybe not give them direct military aid; the Honduran army can take care of that. But, provide them with humanitarian aid." How curious the definition of humanitarian aid which is in vogue in Washington. It includes boots, uniforms, tents, field hospital supplies—the sorts of things that make armies run. The humanitarian aid defined by the Reagan administration is anything that really does not blow up in your face. That's being provided. So, what was the difference between the Reagan administration wanting those supplies, including military ones, to be sent directly into Nicaragua so that contra units could sustain themselves (because they have a lot of trouble sustaining themselves without a significant social base and without those little air drops leaving the fifty-pound boxes of prime steak regularly), and the Democrats saying "No" to that but being willing to keep these people in Honduras intact for the next administration to handle? That is the difference between somebody who wants to come out shooting at you and the other guy that simply wants to put a gun at your head. The two positions are essentially one and the same and are a direct product of the terms of the debate which I think President Reagan has managed to impose on the United States or at least in Washington.

When the recent hurricane ripped through Nicaragua in October 1988, uprooting one out of every ten Nicaraguans, leaving over 185,000 people homeless, destroying many of our crops, mangling more than four hundred miles of road, destroying over thirty bridges, and devastating entire forests causing tremendous ecological damage, we thought that, maybe, for once, politics could have been set aside. Nicaragua thus made an appeal to the entire international community. We understand that the United States is still a member of the international community, although not necessarily a law-abiding one. What was the response? One day after the hurricane hit, we heard Mr. Fitzwater, the White House spokesman, say he was concerned that the relief effort to the Nicaraguans could be used to the detriment of the contras. Two days later, we heard of a proclamation, signed by the president, banning the entry of Nicaraguan government officials or FSLN officials into the country.

We believe it important to have debates, to meet with some of you, and to meet, especially, with groups and organizations in this country that are doing tremendous work in trying to channel relief aid to Nicaragua. Some of the people in California who were involved in the Nicaraguan relief effort were said to have been threatened with prosecution because it occurred to the U.S. governmental authority that they might be able to send generators and certain types of construction materials. They were warned that there was an embargo against Nicaragua. The plane loads, nonetheless, have gotten through. We continue to feel that the best aid that the United States government could give Nicaragua at this moment would be to stop the war and to comply with the sentence of the World Court. This is the best contribution that could be made because it would be a contribution to peace. We would rather have our children hungry than dead.

We think that rationality is going to prevail. We believe in the forces of law and morality here in this country; I have lived here long enough to know that they exist. We are not going to give up on them, and we know that they are going to prevail. We are going through a very difficult period now in Nicaragua. But, I can assure you, we are going to survive. Again, maybe we owe that to President Reagan, too, because he has shown us how to endure, how to organize, how to fight. So our hurricane—by comparison with what we have suffered in the last seven years—maybe is not that much. Heroism, perhaps, is the only commodity in Nicaragua which is not in short supply. No embargo, I believe, is going to put a stop to the flow of American sympathy, of solidary of the American people, and of understanding. As long as the words "morality" and "legality" have any meaning, we believe that common sense is also going to have to prevail over insanity.

9

LIBERAL THINK TANK COMMENT

William Goodfellow

I appreciate the opportunity today to hear from all sides of this debate. As Mr. Bendaña said, in Washington there is rarely any real debate, for we hear from only one side. The Reagan administration has succeeded in defining the terms of the debate. Rather than speaking honestly to the issue, even Democrats who oppose the president's policy begin their speeches with, "Now I don't like the Sandinistas any more than President Reagan does, however. . . ." At that point they already have lost the debate, and are reduced to offering only watered-down versions of the administration's policy.

Although the debates about U.S. policy toward Nicaragua have been one-sided and shallow, they have been plentiful. Contra aid has been the single most divisive foreign policy issue on the congressional agenda over the last eight years. The House has taken more than forty votes on contra aid, and the Senate has voted over twenty times. The debate just drones on and on and on and is rarely enlightening.

In spite of the administration's ability to dominate the debate in Washington, it has not been able to sell the policy to the American people, a majority of whom remain opposed to sending aid to the contras. President Reagan and his foreign policy managers have expended enormous amounts of time and money in an effort to sell the war against Nicaragua to the American people, yet polls indicate that a consistent two-thirds majority of Americans oppose sending aid to the contras; the number jumps to over 90 percent when mention is made of sending U.S. troops to Nicaragua.

Quite simply, the American people do not believe that Nicaragua presents a threat to the United States. Indeed, they wonder why we are sending *any* money to the contras. The average American says, "I don't understand why there is all this fuss over Nicaragua."

Nicaragua seems to be an obsession with this administration. The policy is not logical, for the threat is not real. Most of you in this audience, and I think most of the American people, believe that their government is lying to them. This is not a comfortable position to be in, for one wants to believe in one's government.

Later this afternoon we will hear a discussion of the role of the media. Journalists based in Central America know very well that the administration is lying when they speak of Nicaragua as a "totalitarian dungeon." Any careful reader of the *New York Times* or the *Washington Post* knows that Nicaragua poses no threat to U.S. security. But even our best newspapers are unwilling to stand up day after day and say our government is lying. Whether or not it is conscious, they allow administration assertions to go unchallenged, and allow the administration to set the terms of the debate. For example, enormous coverage has been devoted to the administration's charges of human rights abuses in Nicaragua, but far greater abuses in Guatemala and El Salvador rate barely a mention. The repetition of the same unchallenged charges gives these fabrications a life of their own and distorts the national debate.

Now I would like to address some of the statements made this morning by the gentleman from the State Department, Mr. Witajewski. He spoke of four myths. The first myth, he said, was that Nicaragua was not a threat to anyone. Certainly it is hard to believe that a country that has a half-dozen elevators and three escalators, and not one working jet fighter, is a threat to the security of the United States. What then is the threat?

The Threat of a Good Example

In one sense Nicaragua does represent a threat, a threat to the established order, and that I think goes a long way toward explaining all the fuss. The British aid organization, Oxfam, published a pamphlet about Nicaragua entitled "Threat of a Good Example." In 1979, after the revolution, Nicaragua embarked on ambitious social programs to improve health care and dramatically expand educational opportunities for young and old. Initially these programs met with considerable success. Nicaragua's literacy campaign received worldwide praise. Throughout the Third World Nicaragua was seen as a proving ground

111

for new ideas, for a revolutionary model that was nonaligned, a puppet of neither the Soviet Union nor the United States.

U.S. policy makers felt they could not allow a little country like Nicaragua to defy the United States. Apparently Washington feared that the poor majorities in neighboring countries, in particular Guatemala and El Salvador, might be inspired by Nicaragua's success and might try to follow Nicaragua's example. To make the Nicaraguan example a lot less appealing, the Reagan administration set about systematically destroying the Nicaraguan economy. Today, eight years later, they largely have succeeded.

I would like to call your attention to an important new book on U.S. policy toward Nicaragua. It is entitled *Banana Diplomacy* (New York: Simon and Schuster, 1988) and was written by Roy Gutman, a reporter for the Long Island newspaper *Newsday*. Gutman interviewed key American policy makers and concluded that there were actually two Nicaragua policies: a public policy articulated by the State Department, and a private policy run by the National Security Council, the CIA, and right-wing legislators, particularly Senator Jesse Helms. The public policy was just window dressing to convince Congress and the American people that the administration was pursuing diplomatic efforts to resolve differences with Nicaragua. The real policy, however, had but one objective: ouster of the Sandinistas.

The second myth, according to our friend from the State Department, is that the Sandinistas are involved in a noble experiment. The administration has insisted that the July 1979 Nicaraguan revolution was nothing more than a garden-variety Latin American power grab: no high principles, no concern for the poor; just a small group bent on enriching itself in the time-honored fashion of the Latin *caudillo*. If this is the case, then how do we account for the Reagan administration's obsession with Nicaragua? As I have just suggested, I think the real threat posed by Nicaragua was the example it provided the rest of the undeveloped world, an example that Washington was bent on destroying. The weapons were a trade embargo, a credit embargo, and a proxy war using the contras.

The Economic War

As Mr. Bendaña has just told you, Nicaragua is the only country in Latin America, other than Cuba, that gets no money from the International Monetary Fund (IMF), no money from the World Bank, and no money from the Inter-American Development Bank. He referred to a letter from Secretary of State Shultz to the head of the Inter-American Development Bank, Antonio Ortiz Mena. In his January 1985 letter the secretary of state warned that Congress might cut off U.S. contributions to the bank if the bank went ahead with a proposed $58 million agricultural credit loan to benefit small farmers in Nicaragua. Since the United States contributes nearly half of the Inter-American Development Bank's capital, it has considerable influence. The loan was withdrawn for another "technical review."

Although there are forty-three member nations on the board of the Inter-American Development Bank, the United States, by virtue of its capital contribution and its willingness to throw its weight around, usually prevails. In previous board votes on loans to Nicaragua, the vote count has been forty-two to one, with the United States the sole dissenter.

U.S. opposition to loans to Nicaragua is always couched in economic terms. Secretary Shultz wrote that "the United States continues to be concerned over the focus and direction of Nicaragua's macroeconomic policies." This ruse was necessary because the bank's charter states clearly that "the bank, its officers and employees shall not interfere in the political affairs of any member, nor shall they be influenced in their decisions by the political character of the member or members concerned. Only economic considerations shall be relevant to their decisions."

I was recently in Managua and can attest to the effectiveness of the economic war. Nicaragua is in desperate financial shape. Some blame must be attributed to the Nicaraguan government, but its mistakes account for only a fraction of the chaos that has paralyzed the Nicaraguan economy. The crushing blows have come from the trade embargo, the credit embargo, and from the tremendous resources that the government has had to divert to the military to defend the country against the contra war.

The Sandinista government was scarcely being paranoid when it warned of the danger of a U.S. invasion, especially after the 1983 invasion of Grenada. Key U.S. policy makers, chief among them Assistant Secretary of State for Inter-American Affairs Elliott Abrams, argued hard for an invasion of Nicaragua. The Nicaraguans realized that the Soviets were not going to come to their aid, that they would be on their own. If the United States decided to commit its military forces to an invasion of Nicaragua, there was nothing the Nicaraguan army could do to stop the Americans. They believed, however, that they could reduce the likelihood of an invasion by strengthening Nicaragua's defenses. The Nicaraguan leadership believed that the prospect of high U.S. casualties was a powerful deterrent to an invasion.

Today the Nicaraguan government is spending about half its revenues on the military. This has forced drastic cuts in social expenditures. Most of the early advances in education, health care, and housing have been halted, and in some cases reversed. Even if the war were to end today, it would take a decade to rebuild the country.

Another blow to the economy is the flight of technocrats, of the very people most needed to rebuild the country. It is next to impossible to exist on a Nicaraguan government salary unless one has an additional job in the private sector or is lucky enough to receive remittances from relatives living abroad. Obviously this situation cannot go on forever, and the Nicaraguan government realizes it must come to terms with the United States. They live in our backyard, and they do not have the option of moving to another neighborhood.

U.S.-Nicaraguan Negotiations

Negotiations between the Nicaraguan government and the newly elected Reagan administration in the United States began in the summer of 1981. Over the years the Nicaraguan government has repeatedly offered concessions to the Reagan administration, and each time the administration has upped the ante. In 1984 Nicaraguan President Daniel Ortega offered to sign the fair and balanced Contadora agreement, negotiated by the foreign ministers of Mexico, Panama, Colombia, and Venezuela. Contadora would have accomplished *all* of the stated objectives of the Reagan administration's policy toward Nicaragua, yet the administration moved to block the agreement. In November 1984 the *Washington Post* published a secret National Security Council internal memorandum that boasted, "We have effectively blocked Contadora group efforts to impose the second draft of the revised Contadora Act. . . . We have trumped the latest Nicaraguan/Mexican efforts to rush signature of an unsatisfactory Contadora agreement."

In February 1987 President Oscar Arias of Costa Rica presented his own plan to end the conflicts in Central America. President Arias was hardly a friend of the Sandinistas. Indeed, he did not invite President Ortega to the meeting in Costa Rica where he presented his new plan to the other Central American presidents. Understandably, the

Nicaraguans were initially skeptical. To them it looked like just another effort to isolate Nicaragua. President Arias talked constantly of democratizing Nicaragua, the very same message that was coming from the White House. There was one big difference, however. To Arias, "democracy" meant allowing the Nicaraguan people to elect freely their own leaders; to Reagan, "democracy" was merely the codeword for overthrowing the Sandinistas.

President Arias believed that a fair and open electoral process would democratize Nicaragua regardless of who won. In 1987 he told one of his closest advisers that unless the Sandinistas were willing to undergo a political transformation, "there is no way they could win a free and fair election." However, he was quite willing to see the Sandinistas reelected if they took the steps necessary to make them a truly popular government.

Arias's belief in the benefits of a free and open political process forms the core of the agreement that became known as the Arias plan. The summer of 1987 was a time of intense diplomatic activity in Central America. When it became clear that Costa Rica, Guatemala, and even Nicaragua all seemed to be leaning toward signing Arias's plan, the Reagan administration launched its own diplomatic offensive to scuttle the agreement. Twice a planned summit meeting of the five presidents was postponed as Salvadoran President Napoleon Duarte kept remembering last-minute appointments in Europe. In June, while on a private trip to the United States, President Arias was called to the White House for a meeting with President Reagan and his top foreign policy advisers. Reagan and his lieutenants leaned hard on Arias to modify his plan in a way that would make it unacceptable to the Nicaraguans. Arias held his ground, and finally all five Central American presidents met in Guatemala City on 5 August 1987.

Two days later the presidents of Guatemala, Honduras, El Salvador, Nicaragua, and Costa Rica signed the historic Esquipulas II agreement, still popularly known as the Arias plan. Today, fifteen months later, we can see the results in a more open political process in Nicaragua. The government has declared a general amnesty, freed political prisoners, and restored press freedoms. Perhaps the most concrete accomplishment of the Arias plan to date has been the Sapoá cease-fire agreement between the Nicaraguan government and the contras.

Yesterday Mr. Vendrell talked to you about the report of the International Verification Commission. The commission was made up

115

of the foreign ministers of the five Central American countries and the eight Contadora and support group countries as well as representatives from the UN and OAS. The significance of the verification commission was that, with its Contadora and UN-OAS membership, it was the final mechanism to assure that the plan would be applied evenhandedly.

On 14 January the commission issued what amounts to a report card on the progress each Central American country has made in implementing the Arias plan's provisions. Only Costa Rica was judged to be in complete compliance, but the commission was able to document some progress in each country. Nicaragua was commended for taking concrete steps toward democracy, including reopening the opposition newspaper *La Prensa*. As well, the commission called a cutoff of aid to the contras an indispensable requirement for peace in Nicaragua.

The Contras

Now I would like to address Mr. Witajewski's fourth myth, that the contras do not really want peace. Well, this is true and not true. Half the contras seem to want peace and half do not. This lack of unity has long frustrated U.S. efforts to unite the contras behind a common leadership. Although the contras are a creation of the United States, organized, directed, and funded by the CIA, they have become an unwieldy asset. Their leadership, chosen by the CIA to appeal to Washington, has not been similarly appealing to either the contra rank-and-file or the people of Nicaragua.

Right now there is a split within the contras. One group wants to return to Nicaragua to join the ranks of the legal political opposition. Another group, backed by Elliott Abrams and the CIA, is led by Enrique Bermúdez, a former colonel in Somoza's national guard. This hardline group is holding out for a military victory and is adamantly opposed to anything short of overthrowing the Sandinistas. The group has made it clear that it does not want a negotiated settlement.

The 21 March Sapoá cease-fire agreement between the Nicaraguan government and the contras remains the Arias plan's most concrete achievement, the first agreement between any of the warring parties in Central America. Sapoá must be seen as a first step, for it only suspends the war, it does not end it. Subsequent efforts to reach a permanent cease-fire have faltered.

The last substantive negotiations were held in early June in Managua. Just before the negotiations were scheduled to end, the contras marched into the meeting with a list of new demands, including the right of draftees to leave the army any time they chose, forced resignation of the supreme court, restoration of confiscated property that had been distributed to smallholders and cooperatives, and the opening of contra offices in Managua. The government would have to carry out these actions while the contras retained their arms. The contras gave the government negotiators an ultimatum: they had two hours to accept these demands or the contras would walk out.

Roy Gutman, the author of *Banana Diplomacy*, interviewed Bermúdez and other contra leaders after the June meeting. Bermúdez and his colleagues admitted that as long as the cease-fire negotiations continued, "we had no hope of getting additional [American] aid." Therefore, "we had to take steps to end the negotiations."

Two months ago there was a very short session in Guatemala where Víctor Hugo Tinoco, the Nicaraguan vice-minister of foreign affairs, met with the contras. The two sides could agree on nothing, not even the site of the next negotiating round.

Apparently the contras are dragging their feet in anticipation of a more sympathetic ear in Washington under a Bush administration. No matter who wins the election, George Bush or Michael Dukakis, the contras are unlikely to get additional military aid. The mood in Washington has changed. Congress is not about to reverse itself and vote more military aid for the contras. Those days are over, and the contras had better look for ways to reintegrate themselves into the political process in Nicaragua. What lies ahead, in my opinion, is a long period of what one might call "malevolent neglect." Members of the new administration probably will go through the motions of trying to win more contra aid, but I doubt their heart will be in it. The contras are fast becoming a liability, a disposal problem. Neither a Democratic nor a Republican administration is likely to welcome tens of thousands of contras to Miami.

Advice to the Next President

I think the new administration wisely will turn its attention to more important parts of the world. Although the new foreign policy team probably will continue the past policy of hostility toward Nicaragua, I do not expect Nicaragua to be the obsession that it has been for the Reagan administration.

My unsolicited advice to the next president is to declare victory in Central America. The new president should go before the American people and say, "Our policy has worked. The pressure of the contras and the trade embargo has forced the Nicaraguan government to the negotiating table and it has capitulated. We have won."

Otherwise I see no other way for the next administration to extricate itself from a failed policy. The new president can conveniently leave out the fact that the Nicaraguan government has been willing to negotiate a peace agreement with the United States since 1981. Otherwise it would appear that tens of thousands of Nicaraguan lives and hundreds of millions of American dollars have been wasted.

10

CONSERVATIVE THINK TANK COMMENT

L. Francis Bouchey

There has been a lot of talk of the past at this symposium, and I too shall do some of that. But as a conservative—perhaps the only one here in the room today—I know that the past is a prologue to be built upon, and thus I shall also be speaking this morning about the future. I agree with Professor Wiarda's comment yesterday morning that the United States has lacked a sustained and sophisticated policy of ongoing involvement with Latin America of the sort that we have had with Western Europe and with Japan since the end of World War II.

In Latin America we have oscillated, instead, between intervention and benign neglect. On the other hand, I believe that through sustained involvement on behalf of democratic regimes, we shall lessen the likelihood that intervention, in fact, will be required. In the case of Nicaragua, admittedly, the United States was excessively tolerant of the Somozas. It also failed to support adequately the 1979 OAS mediation which, in the judgment of many who participated in the exercise, could have eased Somoza from power, spared bloodshed, and ushered in a more tranquil era for Nicaragua. That incident is particularly interesting because at that time one of Somoza's best friends—he was often called Somoza's congressman—was John M. Murphy (D-NY) who is now in jail as a result of the Abscam entrapment operation. Mr. Murphy was chairman of the Merchant Marine and Fisheries Committee of the U.S. House of Representatives, which had jurisdiction over the Panama Canal Treaty legislation. Those treaties had received the Senate's "advice and consent" for ratification in April 1978, but they required authorizing, implementing legislation that had to go through the House and through Murphy, who was head of the relevant committee. Mr. Murphy, who

119

had opposed the Carter Torrijos Treaties, advised Carter that if he wanted to see that implementing legislation, he should lay off his friend (Anastasio) Somoza, which, evidently, Mr. Carter did by withdrawing U.S. support from the OAS mediation efforts aimed at securing Somoza's early retirement.

Then, too, it is important to recall intervention or involvement, or lack thereof. I think that the mediation of the OAS was a healthy involvement. In 1979 the uprising which deposed Mr. Somoza was actively and materially aided and assisted by Panama, Venezuela, Costa Rica, and Cuba. The United States was indirectly supportive in that it blocked the resupply of ammunition to Somoza's forces. Sustained involvement in support of democratic development calls for the United States to demand that election results be respected, as was done by Mr. Carter, to his credit, in the case of the Dominican Republic in 1978.

Sustained involvement in support of democratic development also calls for the creation of incentives where possible, and the sustained application of force where necessary. I am convinced that had Congress approved aid to the resistance last February, the Sandinista regime would now be on the ropes or out of the ring altogether. That, in my judgment, would have been a highly desirable state of affairs, both for the Nicaraguan people and for the security interests of the United States.

I do not believe that President Bush will return to benign neglect and abandon the people of Nicaragua to a Marxist-Leninist future. However, the elements of U.S. policy in Central America need to be reconfigured, with diplomacy being given primacy through the launching of a major diplomatic effort aimed at securing Soviet disengagement from Nicaragua and real progress towards a political opening in that country. The resistance, whose morale remains high, in my judgment, should remain in place, but there should be no request for lethal aid until and unless—and I stress "unless" rather than "until"—a diplomatic political settlement with full U.S. involvement fails.

I am troubled by Mr. Bendaña's assertion that the maintenance of the resistance in existence constitutes a crime and constitutes a continued aggression against Nicaragua, because I thought that the Sapoá accords were meant to accommodate the maintenance of those forces in place while the political arrangements were worked out. But, as has been suggested by numerous observers, it appears that the Sandinista objective is the abolition, dismemberment, surrender of the resistance force as a precondition for any talks. And that, I think, does pose difficulty for the initiatives that I would like to see taken.

120

Similarly, it was suggested by Mr. Bendaña that we should seize in 1989 the opportunity that was missed in 1979. My recollection is that Mr. Carter made a very sincere and sustained effort to accommodate the new government in Managua; that substantial direct aid was provided; that more loans were approved for Nicaragua than had been approved in the preceding years; and that, indeed, it was during that period when Nicaraguan sovereignty was exercised in pursuit of a special arrangement with the Soviet Union. I would hope that the Sandinistas would respond to the initiatives which the United States undertook in 1979. Perhaps, given the sorry state of the region, the Sandinistas will respond in a more positive way if the United States undertakes new initiatives in 1989.

The new American president must first insist on direct and explicit linkages in U.S.-U.S.S.R dealings. A truly neutral Nicaragua should be won. Second, the president ought to reconvene the 1984 bipartisan commission on Central America and begin building political support for a major aid package for a pacified Central America. With that underway, he should seek a U.S.-Central American summit.

11

COVERING CENTRAL AMERICA

Fred Kiel

I have been involved in Central America for many years and had some of the best times of my life down there and some of the worst. Like many journalists who have covered the area for any length of time, I have had the unsettling experience of having government and army officials in Guatemala and El Salvador label me a communist. In Nicaragua, I have had officials call me a CIA agent. U.S. embassy officials throughout the region generally treat me and other journalists like slightly wacky relatives who could turn dangerous at any moment. These same officials will praise me as a warm, caring, perceptive guy when I write stories that they think present their viewpoints favorably. Before you ask, I am neither a communist nor a CIA agent; maybe a little wacky.

What is certain is that journalists throughout Central America are considered both potentially dangerous enemies and useful links to Washington and to the American people. The reasons for this are obvious. U.S. influence throughout the world has lessened considerably over the past few decades, but in Central America U.S. power is still overwhelming. Washington's decisions to supply aid to this country's army or that country's guerrilla forces are questions of life or death to them. Leaders of all factions have learned over the past decade that their only recourse to influence Washington is through the media. What has this meant? In practice, this has signified that whether they want it or not, often without even fully understanding why, journalists have become key players in the Central American drama. Everyone tries to sway them, pressure them, or intimidate them. The attempt to influence them comes both from intense, cold-eyed army colonels and from equally intense American nuns and priests who often have the same cold eyes.

There are no neutrals in Central America. This is something a journalist has to learn quickly if he or she is to function effectively in the region. In the States, reporters are trained to interview all sides in a controversy and then to seek outside experts who give their supposedly neutral opinions that will give balance to a story. Well, in the States this does not work as well in practice as in theory; it has almost no validity in Central America.

A few Guatemalans I respected suggested that I speak with this law professor who was instrumental in writing the new civilian constitution. He proved to be a fountain of information on the political intricacies of the situation and delivered them to me in snappy, lively quotes. I assume you all know how journalists love snappy, lively quotes. Then he started to lash out against the Christian Democratic presidential candidate, Vinicio Cerezo, who eventually won the election. I got suspicious and afterwards went back to my Guatemalan contacts, and I said, "Listen, you told me this guy was neutral." They said, "Well, in fact, he does support another presidential candidate and he will get a cabinet post if his man is elected. But he was neutral, or as far neutral as we could see for the Guatemalans that we know."

Now, this brings up another problem that U.S. journalists have to face: the educated, politically active classes are very tiny, practically nonexistent, and are composed of only a few thousand people. We all know this intellectually from reading about it. What it means for a journalist in practice is that he walks into a murky web of intricate political and personal relationships. All the characters themselves understand this, but for a journalist, it is unknown. Everyone is a cousin, related by marriage; their fathers were best friends in relation-ships that could go back generations. Yet, two people tied this way could still be bitter political enemies. Americans just are not used to this type of situation.

I will give you another example. I had a Guatemalan girlfriend whose father was an army colonel. Back in the late 1960s, during the first guerrilla war, he was strolling along a Pacific beach on vacation. From the other direction, on the shore, he saw a top Marxist guerrilla leader. Did the colonel tackle him? Did he shout for police? He just nodded and smiled as they crossed paths. Why? It turns out that they were longtime friends. The guerrilla leader was a former army officer himself, and he had been through cadet school with this colonel. The colonel told his daughter, "What could I do? We were both on vacation." But vacations ended and both men were killed in separate combats within a year.

This kind of chivalry does not usually reign in Central America. It is usually the complete opposite. As news director for United Press, I have had to make emergency trips several times over the past six years to pull out correspondents who were hiding in embassies or in friends' houses under death threats or just with their nerves physically wrecked because of the strains of reporting under the situations that existed. In one particularly nasty example, a Salvadoran army colonel, who was in charge of press relations, came up to Washington where he made a tour of media headquarters in attempts to improve the image of the Salvadoran army. He gave his spiel in English to the UPI executives. When they departed and he was left alone in the room with a Latin American news editor who is Argentinean, he switched to Spanish and said, "Listen, your Salvadoran correspondent is meeting with guerrillas. We can tell you the times, the places, and the names of the people he is meeting with. We want you to know that he is either with us or against us."

Well, the Latin American editor informed the other executives who, as you can imagine, were pretty stirred up by this whiff of menace and violence coming up out of the Potomac at them. They called me up and asked me to fly there immediately to assess the situation, to see whether it was safe for the Salvadoran correspondent to continue. I flew to San Salvador and met with the colonel after he returned and with the top brass in the army. I explained to them in conversations which went on for many hours that a reporter has to interview not only Salvadoran officers to find out what great fighters they are, how they are gentle with widows and orphans, but also with government officials, opposition politicians, and guerrillas, if we can. That is just a part of our job. Grudgingly, they accepted this, and I am happy to say that the Salvadoran reporter is still working for us, still pretty safe.

The Salvadoran colonel was not as lucky. As an aside, about a year later, his concept of either with us or against us caught up with him on a San Salvador tennis court. He was dressed in his whites, waiting to play. A guerrilla hit team came up, shot him in the head, and then draped his body with the FMLN flag. That is the picture that went out to the world. It is one of the more noteworthy pictures that have come out of the horrible war.

There are similar, more well-known examples of how the small political classes act in each country. In Salvador, I am sure you all know about José Napoleón Duarte and Guillermo Ungo, how they were on the same presidential ticket in 1972. Ten years later, Duarte was with the government and Ungo supported the guerrillas. Or note the Chamorro family in Nicaragua, where different members edit the two pro-Sandinista newspapers and the others *La Prensa*, the opposition.

This brings up another fact, that there are no neutral local journalists in Central America. There is just no tradition for neutrality. The journalists are engaged, the newspapers are all engaged, for one side or another. UPI, like other news agencies and other news organizations, uses local reporters in each of the countries—either as stringers or as backup—for our correspondence. They are very useful as long as you understand their points of view and their sensibilities. They cause a lot of grief if you forget that and seemingly trample their sensibilities. In Honduras we had an American correspondent, I will call him Larry. He was doing a good job for us, getting us exclusive stories on the links between the Honduran military and the contras before such links became public knowledge. Larry worked out of our office at *el Tiempo* newspaper, which is perhaps the best in Honduras. But it is also a fierce opponent of U.S. military involvement in the region and of the alleged subservience of the Honduran military to the U.S. and of the Honduran military assistance to the contras. Larry should have gotten along well in this environment, but he irritated the Honduran journalists with what they considered to be his superior American attitude and they got him for it.

December 28 is *el dia de los inocentes* in much of Latin America, that is the Day of the Innocents, or their equivalent of April Fool's Day. The night before one 28th of December, *el Tiempo* reporters called Larry over and said, "Come on, look here, we've got a hot scoop in tomorrow's newspapers," and they showed him a story supposedly exposing some of the dealings involving the U.S. ambassador, saying that the Honduran government would ask for his recall. This article ended with the greeting that is normal in these yearly spoofs "Happy Day of the Innocents." This clued the reader in that the entire story was made up, that the *el Tiempo* editors—all anti-Reagan—were just indulging in some good-natured, wishful thinking. Now, Larry had heard of the Day of the Innocents but he just did not connect it in his mind to this story, and he did not read the final sentence. No one bothered to tell him. You either knew or you did not know, they thought. He filed the story the next day. He did try to get comment from the U.S. embassy but the public affairs officer, since it was so early, had not yet read the article, and just gave him a no comment. So, Larry's headline came out, "U.S. Ambassador to be Expelled from Honduras." Well, this ambassador failed to see the humor in either story, in *el Tiempo*'s or UPI's.

There is something about working for a wire agency that newspaper reporters do not have to confront, and that is that U.S. embassies and also government agencies in Central America—like the Nicaraguan Foreign Ministry and the Panamanian military—are all clients and they receive the stories the same day, as soon as they hit the wire. This meant that there was a State Department protest in our Washington headquarters before lunch that day which did not do much for the appetites of my bosses. We investigated and had to retract the story. They wanted to fire Larry for that but before that process was completed, the Honduran government expelled him. There are two lessons in this: journalists should never be as gullible as Larry was, and at the same time they have to show respect to Central Americans.

Coming from a powerhouse country of 240 million people and going down to a tiny and poor agricultural country, it is sometimes too easy to slip into that mode, you know, that we come from a superior civilization. The Central Americans are all too ready to pick up on this, are looking for it, and are all too ready to play the American—whether he is a journalist, diplomat, businessman, or academic—as the foolish innocent. In Central America, everyone wants to use journalists. They want to use them or get rid of them. Journalists always have to remember that.

It is true that nowadays Central American officials, businessmen, and academics are fairly accessible to foreign correspondents. Reporters can now roam where they want in the countryside except for some exceptions in Honduras and Nicaragua. This is a major improvement over the early 1980s when many officials, especially army officers, considered correspondents to be foreign devils, and if you arrived unannounced someplace in the boondocks, you were likely to have a squad of rifles pointed at you. What this now means, though, is that journalists can get much more information out of Central America, much more easily. They can go into the countryside and report on the social developments or lack thereof, on the economic deterioration that is occurring in so many regions, on the fighting where it still occurs, and on the peasants, who, as always, take the brunt of everything.

126

However, all this pleasant cooperation breaks down completely when a real crisis explodes. There are several reasons for this. In the first hours, the first days of a crisis, no one really knows the entire picture. Here is where I could understand how officials could come to hate reporters because they get to be like yapping dogs wanting to know everything immediately when it just is impossible. Then public relations and political considerations take over. Officials will lie or mislead, trying to put the best face on the situation. Then they will take what they consider to be the prudent course; they will cut reporters off from access to the crisis zone. They are afraid of what the reporters will find—something they do not know or something they do not want exposed.

One of the most vivid and cynical uses of journalists that I have experienced in Central America took place in April 1986. This was one of the periodic "Nicaraguan raids on Honduras" scares, which, as you know, generally pop up when the Reagan administration wants more contra aid voted in Congress. Neither side here was innocent except, again, any peasants who may have gotten caught in the cross fire. The Sandinistas knew about the upcoming vote in Congress, yet they used the period right before to try and deliver a knockout blow to the contras by attacking their main military training camp inside Honduras where there were hundreds of raw recruits not yet armed. The camp was defended, of course.

Washington reacted by saying this was a threat to Honduran sovereignty and offered emergency military assistance as well as helicopters to ferry in Honduran troops to the border. Well, in Central America, not much goes right; even the most efficient Washington bureaucrats can stumble down there when they try to coordinate any sort of action. From Mexico we asked our local reporters to talk to the Honduran military and to the government. They said, "Nope, there's no invasion, we don't know anything about Sandinistas crossing." Even the U.S. embassy in Tegucigalpa in the first day failed to get the word, and they also denied there was any large-scale invasion. The result was that UPI Washington was putting out scare stories with statements from the Reagan administration and the Honduran ambassador to Washington saying that the Sandinista juggernaut was advancing deep into Honduras, while UPI Honduras was putting out stories saying, "What? What invasion?" Eventually, Washington got everyone on board and there was a full-blown crisis. The line was this: the thin line of Honduran soldiers fighting valiantly against the Sandinista invasion.

127

I would like to go into a bit of detail on this one because I think it illustrates what a journalist has to put up with in Central America, when he is swamped with lies and half-truths, cut off from all access to the crisis zone, and still expected to come up with some sort of an accurate picture of what is going on.

On the days leading up to this crisis I was in beautiful Costa Rica, covering a placid economic conference and having a fine time. Then I got the word that I had to go to Honduras, which is beautiful but not one of the liveliest places in the world. So I was doubly grumpy when I had to get up at 4:00 A.M. to catch a dawn flight. From there we were directed straight to the U.S. embassy in Tegucigalpa where I met dozens of other newly arrived journalists who were just as confused as I was. But the fact that the Honduran officials sent us all to the U.S. embassy gave us some kind of indication of who was running things for this particular crisis. We were bombarded with briefings inside the embassy by U.S. military officials with crisp uniforms and by civilian intelligence officers. They had beautiful maps. I remember the black arrows showing the Sandinista thrusts, other arrows showing the contra counterthrusts, and still another showing how we were ferrying Honduran troops to the border. It was all pretty impressive.

The reporters, as one, said, "We want to go to the combat zone to see the supposed big invasion." Conveniently, it was too dangerous for us. Let me tell you, concern over our safety is not a prime consideration of U.S. embassy officials, but they offered to take us to see the Hondurans in action. At the same time we were being bombarded from our headquarters in the States saying, "We need datelines from the border." It was a huge crisis out of Washington. Also, they wanted things like, "What are the Hondurans in Tegucigalpa doing? Are they stocking up on food, are they fleeing to the hills?" Of course, absolutely nothing was happening in Tegucigalpa, which was normal.

Then, it was off to the border in U.S. military choppers that went bouncing and swooping up and around and between mountains and valleys, dips and everything, supposedly to evade the Sandinista missiles, or the possibility thereof. But, of course, some of us thought it was to get as many reporters as air sick as possible. Once we landed, there were hundreds of Honduran soldiers everywhere, strolling around peacefully, unconcerned. It was obvious that they were not going into or out of combat. There, a gung-ho Honduran colonel, grenades strapped to his vest, gave us another briefing, showing us maps where the Honduran troops were chasing the Sandinistas who supposedly were scurrying back across the border out of fear of the Hondurans. Now, the reporters really got on him. We were only thirty miles away, but there were no roads. The only way we could get there was by them because it was all mountains; thirty miles but, I would say, a three-day hike because of the mountains. "Take us. We want to see the Hondurans in action, fighting. It's our job."

The colonel gave us the same excuse that the Americans did: "It's too dangerous; but wait," he said, "you're in great luck, a chopper is coming in with some dead Sandinistas; this is proof that we're fighting them." Sure enough a chopper came and landed, oh, about one hundred yards away, dumped off a few bloated bodies of youths, faces covered with flies. The youths did have on Sandinista camouflage uniforms. The cameras clicked. We had to interview the Hondurans, who said, "Yeah, we killed them." It was a staged photo opportunity but we had to do it.

At the same time in Managua, Sandinista officials, including Daniel Ortega, were issuing strong denials that they had made any kind of incursion into Honduras. The contra leaders, who were usually so eager to meet with the media—they love secret rendezvous in Honduran hotels; that's their forte—had disappeared completely, were nowhere to be found. This story was a real maze to cover. The only thing we could do was to put into our articles as many disclaimers as possible, with the main fact that we were not allowed into the crisis region, and also linking it as tightly as possible to the upcoming vote in Congress on contra aid.

From all the heat generated in the first few days of the crisis—heat or hot air, depending on your point of view—we thought we would be in Honduras for weeks. On a Saturday afternoon, however, the embassy just rang the curtain down on this performance. Boom! Just like that. They came out from their offices and said, "The crisis is over; the Sandinistas are gone. There will be no more briefings; there will be no more free trips to the border. The Hondurans have closed off the border. Go home."

The real story did come out in the following months. The Sandinistas admitted that they had attacked the training school inside Honduras, "The headquarters of our enemies. So what?" U.S. officials off the record admitted that there had been no real threat to Honduran sovereignty. As for the contras, they laughed over their experiences: how they had been asked to get some dead Sandinistas that they had killed and turn them over to the Hondurans so the Hondurans could show them to us as an example of their military prowess.

This is the world in which journalists operate in Central America, being lied to or pressured from all sides and often cut off from access to the site where things happen. We function best when we can get to the scene, when we can interview witnesses and participants in these events. This is old-fashioned, basic journalism but these opportunities do occur and you have to recognize them and seize them.

A few years ago, a U.S. army chopper was shot down over the Nicaraguan-Honduran border, crash landed inside Honduras, just inside the border, and the American pilot was shot to death because he tried to escape. The other crew members escaped. "We didn't do it," the Sandinistas said from Managua, "Maybe it was those trigger-happy Hondurans." The Hondurans denied it, "We didn't do it; we just stood around and watched," which is exactly what they did.

In Washington, they put out statements about (this is not a direct quote) "cold-blooded Sandinista murder," implying that the chopper was flying peacefully over Honduran air space. I was in Mexico and I called our American correspondent in Managua and said, "What do you think?" He said, "Didn't you see the story I filed on the Nicaraguan denial?" I told him, "Look, everybody's denying everything. Why don't you go to the frontier yourself and see?" He resisted. He said, "The Sandinistas have already denied it. Why would they do something so stupid as shooting down a U.S. chopper, which might provoke Reagan to bomb who knows what?" He said, "The frontier is probably closed off anyway."

Well, I was the boss. He went and he was happy that he did. He got an exciting story, a great story on the split-second decisions that mean life or death in Central America. We were lucky in that most Sandinista officers had been withdrawn from the border area, probably to be debriefed. This left behind just the soldiers who were involved in the incident. They were mostly teenagers and anxious to tell the story of all the excitement. They told our man how the chopper came from Honduras, crossed the border—it's not really a very well-marked border but they all knew where it was—came flying until it was practically overhead, well inside their territory, and they opened up on it. They opened up with all their rifles and antiaircraft machine guns and kept on shooting it as it turned, crash-landed inside Honduras, and they just kept on shooting. So, the Nicaraguans almost certainly had international law on their side but they still denied it in Managua—again, over the need to sway U.S. opinion. Over the years, almost everyone has learned that it's just not nice to kill Americans down there. So, this is old-fashioned reporting, digging. If we had accepted the versions of either side, or all sides, to put something together, it would not have been nearly as accurate. However, you all know that journalism is not meant to give the definitive version of any incident, of any epic, only the searing first impression.

It is true that in the early 1980s a lot of inexperienced reporters flocked down to Central America. They all wanted to expose another Vietnam or they were too young to report from Vietnam and they wanted to report a war. They thus turned it into a situation that one U.S. embassy official called "a kindergarten for foreign correspondents." It is true the Stateside editors failed to understand how important Central America would be, failed to comprehend the obsession of the Reagan administration with the region, and allowed this situation to go on for too long. Most of this has ended. The media now sends in experienced people. These are not their first jobs in journalism. They are not easily swayed. They want to see for themselves.

In this respect, U.S. journalism is almost unique in the area. "Almost" because there are exceptions. I found that West European and Latin American reporters go into Central America with a much better in-depth understanding of the history and culture of the region, but with ideological baggage that often taints their objectivity. I have seen them and heard their questions, observed how they will look for information to fit their world view, whether it is of the left or of the right.

American journalists, on the whole, have open minds. That is not to say that they are objective; who can be totally objective? But they have open minds. Sometimes they get hoodwinked; sometimes they are describing an elephant's hindquarters when they think they are holding onto an attractive face. But, on the whole, they strive for accuracy despite all the obstacles strewn in their path.

Finally, there are so many Americans down there nowadays, each with his own set of beliefs and prejudices, that no single version of what is taking place in Central America reaches the American people: not the Washington point of view, not the Sandinista point of view, not any single point of view, but many points of view. I prefer it that way.

12

A CRITIQUE OF U.S. MEDIA COVERAGE
OF CENTRAL AMERICA

Jeff Cohen

Now Fred talked a lot about the process of reporting about Central America, especially from Central America. I am going to talk about something slightly different. That is the media product. At the group that I head, known as FAIR, we consume an awful lot of print, and we watch an awful lot of television. If you had to watch as much television as I have to, I think you would develop the same method of operation that we have at FAIR; we laugh to keep from crying.

I want to begin my little talk today with a two-word joke, Geraldo Rivera. His is one of the few programs to which I have not been invited. I have decided that there is a reason for it: I do not worship Satan, I am not a transvestite police officer, nor am I a Nazi skinhead. I have been on Mort[on] Downey's TV show and radio show, however. I remember when I was on his radio show once during the "Amerika" (with a K) miniseries controversy. That was the Soviet conquest of America. He introduced the program this way: "With me on the phone from Washington, D.C., is the conservative, Reed Irvine, and for the other side we thought we would get the view of Moscow; but we thought we could save money on our phone bill by just calling New York City, and on with me from New York City is Jeff 'Leonid' Cohen." Now my response was instantaneous: "Always nice to be with you Mort 'Joe McCarthy' Downey. I can count on you to try to smear your opponent before he even gets a chance at your audience at his opening remarks."

Now, I want to turn to my criticism of the mainstream media, especially the television networks and such quality media as the *New*

York Times and the *Washington Post*. Because you could argue that the coverage of Central America during the Reagan era, in many ways, has been a national joke in the way that Geraldo Rivera is. I want to begin by raising some questions about objectivity in the media.

Objective reporting, in my view, does not necessarily have much to do with providing a fair or accurate view of the world. In the early twentieth century in this country, as you know, journalism did not pretend to be objective. It was partisan. You could attack political figures you did not like, political parties you did not like, and foreign governments you did not like. You could do that in a news story. Near the lead of the story, you could have written (if the old convention held today), "Nicaragua is a totalitarian dungeon bent on expanding its atheistic communism to the democratic neighbors of El Salvador, Guatemala, and Honduras."

Now, that would be inappropriate. You could never get away with that lead. But you could write, "'Nicaragua is a totalitarian dungeon bent on expanding its atheistic communism to the democratic neighbors of Honduras, Guatemala, and El Salvador,' the Reagan administration said in a speech today." Those extra words make it objective reporting. It makes it appropriate reporting. Why? Because it is sourced to someone in power. It is appropriate because the reporters could say they did not inject their opinion into the story. It is appropriate even if everything the source—in this case, President Reagan—said was false. And it's appropriate journalism even without the statement, "The president's claims could not be verified."

We have hunted through *New York Times* stories—dozens and dozens and dozens of them—without ever finding reservations about the unverifiability of the president's claims. It would not only be appropriate reporting, I believe it would be typical reporting; as typical, for example, as the *New York Times'* coverage in 1986, which is basically journalism by White House denunciation. I would refer people to Tom Walker's book, the chapter about the media written by Jack Spence ["The U.S. Media: Covering (Over) Nicaragua," in *Reagan Versus the Sandinistas: The Undeclared War on Nicaragua*, ed. Thomas Walker (Boulder: Westview Press, 1987)]. Jack Spence refers to this as "broken record journalism." Every day we hear a different accusation, from Reagan one day, Shultz the next, Reagan again, Abrams the next, Shultz again, and a constant repetition of the story and the line, which often are lies. Obviously the bias of objective journalism depends on the bias of one's sources.

133

Approximately 80 percent of the sources of foreign policy news stories in the U.S. media are U.S. officials, usually from the executive branch—the White House, the Department of Defense, the Department of State, and the Central Intelligence Agency. The problem with the Central American coverage is that so much of it does not emanate at all from Central America or events happening in Central America. It emanates from actions, statements, or lies that come out of Washington, D.C. The television networks do not even have bureaus in Central America, but they do have mobs of journalists who are ready to transmit anything that the White House says, even if they have to scream over the noise of a helicopter. Professor Ed Herman of the Wharton School studied *New York Times'* coverage for a few months in 1984, around the time of the El Salvador election and the Nicaragua election. In studying those news sources, he found that when it came to El Salvador election stories in the *New York Times*, almost all of them were based on U.S. and Salvadoran government sources. As for stories about the Nicaraguan election, on the other hand, more than 80 percent of the sources were U.S. officials or the right-wing opposition faction in Nicaragua that was boycotting the election.

As a result of the sources chosen, the reported stories were pretty obvious and predictable. The stories about Nicaragua's elections focused on the election boycott. The stories about the Salvadoran election, because they did not have the critical sources, have very few references about why the Salvadoran left had decided not to participate in that election. The biased selection of sources I think leads to the bias in the stories.

Moreover, Herman noticed that certain issues were appearing in certain stories and not in the others. In other words, the issues of press freedom and limits on candidates were never discussed in the articles about the El Salvador election, but they appeared in most of the stories about the Nicaraguan election.

Given this heavy reliance on government sources and virtually no reliance on critical sources, I think the mainstream media are ripe targets for government manipulation, even hoaxes. It began early in this administration in 1981 with the phantom Libyan hit squads that were allegedly stalking President Reagan. It turns out that was probably disinformation from William Casey. Then the Soviet MIGs [about to arrive in Nicaragua on election day in 1984]—they were phantoms as well. That source was probably the Office of Public Diplomacy and Oliver North. In 1985, you had the hoax about an upswing in Libyan terrorism that would be aimed at Western Europe. That was an admitted disinformation hoax from Admiral Poindexter. In spite of all of the Caseys and Norths and Poindexters, my favorite source of information to the news media on Central America has always been Otto Reich. How many people have ever heard of him? The *Miami Herald* had a little story about Otto Reich: "You may not know Reich, but you know his work." Otto Reich headed the Office of Public Diplomacy, which nominally was connected to the U.S. State Department, but was actually run out of the National Security Council. There is a great article in the Fall 1988 issue of *Foreign Policy*. It exposes this White House propaganda operation aimed at the media first and then at the American public. Reich's job, in short, was to plant stories with malleable reporters about Nicaragua or to intimidate independent reporters. His propaganda goal was always the same: to magnify the "Nicaragua threat." That office was responsible for the Soviet MIGs hoax. A lot of disinformation was planted in the media. One was a story (I believe Oliver North worked on this one) that the Nicaraguans had acquired chemical weapons. Does anybody know when Oliver North ever slept? That's the question.

The Office of Public Diplomacy (OPD) planted a story on the front page of the *Washington Times*, which was sourced to a "classified U.S. government document," that said the Sandinista government had massacred fifty political prisoners. That was based on a cable which, it turned out, was asking if an allegation from a single Nicaraguan peasant should be investigated. That cable was given to a bunch of journalists, who turned it down, but it was front-page news in the *Washington Times*. The OPD put out this government propaganda, using a butchered quote from Tomás Borge: "The revolution goes beyond our borders. Our revolution was always internationalist." What the government did not tell us is that the quote had a missing part which further stated, "This does not mean we support their revolution. It is sufficient that they take our example." In spite of the fact that this was an office basically set up to spin, twist, distort, and disinform, when the *Miami Herald* did an expose about Otto Reich, interviewing twelve State Department reporters, they found that these reporters were continually going back to Otto Reich and his office for more information.

I want to read from a declassified document, that is, one from the Office of Public Diplomacy to Patrick Buchanan. Patrick Buchanan, at the time, was the White House communications director. What is significant about this is that it boasts of all sorts of media manipulation.

Every time I hear Patrick Buchanan attacking the left-wing media, I have to laugh, because no one knows better than Patrick Buchanan the way the media was twisted over the events in Central America. This was a report to Buchanan about what the office had done in one short week.

It talked about helping an Op-Ed piece get written and placed in the *Wall Street Journal*. It talked about helping Fred Francis at NBC News put out a piece that was considered "a positive piece from the perspective of the White House and the Office of Public Diplomacy"; about taking the contra leaders on tour of different media; about writing Op-Ed pieces under the signatures, under the bylines, of Alfonso Robelo, Adolfo Calero, and Arthuro Cruz. The end of the report talks about a cable from the State Department and it is sort of a boast. It ends, "Do not be surprised," Buchanan was told, "if this cable somehow hits the evening news."

Now, what is important about the Office of Public Diplomacy's operation was that it involved CIA propaganda experts. It recruited people from the Defense Department who were specialists in psychological warfare, and, in the words of a U.S. official quoted in the *Miami Herald*, what they were doing was "a vast psychological warfare operation of the kind the military conducts to influence a population in enemy territory." Of course, the target of this operation was the U.S. population.

One of the pieces of disinformation about Central America that did not emanate from Washington, D.C., came from Coral Gables, Florida. The reason we know that is that we know one of the individuals who were there when this hoax was originated and we have interviewed him. His name is Edgar Chamorro, the former PR person for the contras. Chamorro said that in the spring of 1983 he gathered with three CIA officials at Coral Gables, trying to plan something that would really hurt the Nicaraguans in the media. They decided that a story about the Sandinistas being an anti-Semitic regime that persecuted and harassed Nicaraguan Jews would go over big. It did play big in the U.S. media. Chamorro later told the *Boston Globe* (after he quit the contras), "It was just a propaganda thing. They—the CIA agents—said the media was controlled by Jews, and if we could show Jews were being persecuted, that would help a lot."

Of course, many other factors in faulty news coverage about Central America go beyond government manipulation. One of those factors is that many reporters and editors share the same cold war biases

136

as the White House. Those reporters and editors who do not share those biases are often the victims of intimidation or harassment. In fact, Raymond Bonner, who used to be at the *New York Times*, has talked about the fear independent reporters have of being labeled "soft on communism." Ray Bonner ought to know. He was writing stories for the *New York Times* from El Salvador, writing about atrocious human rights violations, and linking the crimes to the Salvadoran government, which, at the time, the Reagan administration said was a fledgling democracy. What the Reagan administration and its right-wing allies did was to run a six-month campaign to get Ray fired. It included meeting with the publisher of the *New York Times*, Mr. Sulzberger. In October 1982, after all of this pressure, Accuracy in Media, a McCarthyite right-wing organization, could boast in its newsletter, "Some good news! You can quit writing Mr. Sulzberger at the *New York Times* about Raymond Bonner. Bonner is no longer a correspondent for the *Times* in Central America." Bonner was a lesson to other reporters about straying and becoming too independent. It is a lesson you will still hear talked about by people in El Salvador who have been covering El Salvador, and they all remember what happened to Ray Bonner.

Moving to a broader issue, the Reagan administration, I believe, has shown great adeptness at focusing reporters' attentions on human rights abuses in so-called enemy governments in the East bloc and Nicaragua, while packaging these other countries—Guatemala, Salvador, Honduras—always as fledgling democracies—ever, ever fledgling.

To bring this point home, note that in 1984 one of the biggest stories in the news was the abduction and assassination of the activist priest in Poland, Jerzy Popieluszko. It was a major story for months in the TV networks. In the very first week of that story, ninety column inches were given in the *New York Times*. On the other hand, looking to a "fledgling democracy," over a dozen Guatemalan priests were assassinated in the early 1980s; this was almost totally ignored by the news media. A Catholic missionary, Felipe Balán Tomas, was abducted while saying mass—virtually at the same time that the Polish priest was abducted—and there was not even one inch of it in the *New York Times*.

When I speak to general audiences about media bias, I ask for a show of hands: how many people are familiar with a newspaper called *La Prensa*? Even in a general audience, most of the hands go up. Then I ask, how many of you are familiar with the newspaper *La Crónica del Pueblo*? No hands ever go up. How about *El Independiente*? No hands go up. There is a reason for that. It is not the fault of the public.

You can look at the *New York Times* and see that the plight of *La Prensa* [of Nicaragua] has been a major raging story. We looked back at *New York Times* stories and found as of about a year ago over sixty *New York Times* stories that had a focus on *La Prensa*. What about the other two papers I mentioned? Those were two Salvadoran papers in the early 1980s that were violently exterminated. *La Crónica* was closed after the managing editor and photographer were hacked to death. *El Independiente* was bombed twice, and the editors were arrested, killed, or exiled. We looked in the *New York Times* and found a total of three references to the closure of these two newspapers. It is something that continues today. In June of 1988, *La Prensa* was closed for fifteen days—major coverage. Virtually the same week, *La Epocha* in Guatemala was bombed and was closed for much more than fifteen days. Does anyone know if *La Epocha* is even open now? I do not think it is open; that story was virtually ignored.

Why is media suppression more of a story in Nicaragua than it is elsewhere? In recent years, beginning in 1979, over seventy journalists were killed by the state or allied death squads in Guatemala or El Salvador. Those are the fledgling democracies. That figure is according to the Committee to Protect Journalists out of New York. No journalists have been executed by the government of Nicaragua or allied forces.

La Prensa is a special obsession of mine. The closing of any newspaper should, of course, offend any civil libertarian, and I am one of those card-carrying members of the ACLU. The coverage of *La Prensa*, however, is a little bit outrageous. It borders on puffery that gets to the point of absurdity. In many ways, that newspaper can be compared to our *National Enquirer*. It has had stories about women giving birth to chickens, but it gets puff coverage from the U.S. media. The *Washington Post* has written glowing editorials. The thing that we found to be the epitome of what I am talking about was a reference in the *Christian Science Monitor* (12 March 1987) to Pedro Joaquín Chamorro, Sr., as the independent editor of *La Prensa* who "strongly opposed the Somosa and Sandinista regimes." That's a tough one because Chamorro, Sr., had been assassinated before there was a Sandinista regime. At any rate, puffery sometimes gets the best of itself.

Obviously the media strategy of the Reagan administration is to shift media attention to every real or imagined peccadillo in Nicaragua and away from the far worse human rights situations in El Salvador,

138

Guatemala, or Honduras. Why do I say they are far worse? Because I have checked objective experts, such as Amnesty International and Americas Watch, as opposed to checking Elliott Abrams and the State Department. It is amazing how successful the administration has been in shifting attention to Nicaragua. You could say, in many ways, Reagan's Nicaragua obsession has become the media's Nicaragua obsession. What we did to verify this was to the check coverage very closely from the day the regional peace accord was signed in August 1987. We analyzed all of the *New York Times* coverage—215 articles. And we looked at how much of it was about Nicaragua and how much of it was about these other countries. For every one column inch about El Salvador, we found five column inches about Nicaragua. For every one column inch about Honduras, we found twenty-two inches about Nicaragua. For every one column inch about Guatemala, we found twenty-six times the coverage about Nicaragua. The *San Francisco Bay Guardian* did a similar study involving the *New York Times* and seven other dailies. They found this very same pattern.

What was the coverage during that ninety days when it was focused so heavily on Nicaragua? Can Nicaragua be trusted to negotiate? Can they be trusted to comply with the agreement? Has Nicaragua gone far enough? Anyone with eyes open at that time knew that there was one government that was basically turning its nose at the agreement, and that was Honduras. Honduras refused even to appoint a national reconciliation commission. It refused to acknowledge that its territory was the home of insurgent forces fighting in Nicaragua—the contra bases. Yet, for every one inch about Honduras, there were twenty-two inches about Nicaragua.

The double standard played itself out, not just quantitatively, but qualitatively. A week after the signing, two right-wing lawyers were arrested at a demonstration in Managua. Huge media play! The incident was cited repeatedly as proof that Nicaragua would not abide by a regional peace accord. A few weeks later, a group of high school students in El Salvador was arrested for distributing illegal leaflets. The students were tortured with electric shock. One of them stayed in custody for months. This story received virtually no mention in the mainstream media. We could not find it in the *San Francisco Bay Guardian*'s hunt of eight dailies. When you compare what was going on during the ninety-day period in which we were checking the *New York Times*' coverage, in El Salvador there were all these newsworthy things happening: the head of the human rights commission was murdered, a union leader disappeared, the two high school students were abducted, and forty-five hundred Salvadoran refugees came back from Honduras whom the army did not permit the archbishop to go and visit. So there were all these things happening in El Salvador that did not get covered while the obsession was on Nicaragua.

When we confront mainstream media people about this disparity, their answer is, "Come on, U.S. policy makes Nicaragua the biggest story in the region. It's purely because of U.S. policy." Well, the fallacy in that is that U.S. policy pretty much tells the government of Honduras what to do. U.S. policy is responsible for the Salvadoran government. Indeed, it is possible that we spend more American taxpayers' money in the Salvador policy than we do in Nicaragua. In fact, most of the Salvadoran budget comes from U.S. tax money. The situation has everything that the news media usually require for newsworthiness in a story. If you know television, the motto at most television stations is, "If it bleeds, it leads." Television is very big on urban violence. El Salvador has a lot of urban violence and it just does not get the coverage that Nicaragua is getting.

Let me move from the quantity of the coverage to some of the quality, and let me shortcut this because I am probably running late. Many of you have received our questionnaire for the *New York Times*. The *New York Times*, by the way, has not answered the questionnaire. We asked very specific things: Why, when the mothers of political prisoners gathered in Nicaragua and their event was disrupted, did that receive prominent page-five coverage and a photograph, but when mothers of political prisoners gathered in San Salvador and the march was attacked by riot police, the incident was totally ignored by the *New York Times*? Why, when two leaders of the opposition in Honduras were assassinated, was that event buried on a back page, given a total of five paragraphs, 160 words, but a few days later, when some oppositionists were arrested in Nicaragua and detained for a total of seven hours, the incident received front-page coverage above the fold? And we went on and on in asking them for explanations.

I want to talk a little bit about the ability of the Reagan administration to manipulate headlines. I think it has shown an amazing ability. We have been somewhat horrified watching. By "headline news," I am talking about what leads on the national network news and what gets on the front pages. Obviously the killing of Guatemalan priests and religious workers has never been such a story. The aerial bombing and displacement of peasants in El Salvador has never been such a story.

Yet, when Ronald Reagan hoists a photograph that purports to show the Sandinistas are dealing drugs, it is headline and front-page news for days. When the State Department puts out a "White Paper" about El Salvador saying that the Salvadoran insurgency is the result of an international communist plot in essence, that is front page news. Grabbing the headlines with scare stories about foreign enemies is exactly what this administration's media strategy has been, and it has succeeded. If inquiring reporters later poke around and they find that this headline story which dominated the news for a few days turns out to be a hoax, the Reagan administration does not really care because it can count on the truth to come out weeks later on the back page, too little, too late. In fact, Napoleon made a statement that you do not have to suppress the news altogether, you just have to delay it until it matters no longer. That is exactly what the Reagan administration has done. The classic case is the Salvadoran "White Paper."

This was put out as soon as the Reagan administration took power. It alleged a global communist plot arming the Salvadorans; it got headline news; the National Security Council approved $65 million in emergency funds to the Salvadoran government, which was then a government by death squads. Weeks later, John Dingus, in a column in the *L.A. Times*, began to poke holes in it, and then Jonathan Kwitny, the great reporter who used to be at the *Wall Street Journal*, had a story in which he got the author of the report to admit, "Yeah, it was an embellishment, it was a spin, it was an exaggeration." But the Reagan administration did not care because the money was already flowing and the intervention was already upgraded. It repeated this successful formula over and over and over with the Libyan hit squads, the Soviet MIGs, and the Grenada airlines that were going to be sending their planes to bomb Athens, Ohio. When I confronted Ted Koppel once on a national ABC "Viewpoint" show, he told me sort of sternly, "Mr. Cohen, journalists deal in facts, not truth. Truth is left to the historians." I would argue that the role of media is also to deal with facts, and with a little more skepticism they could deal in a lot more facts.

Let me start winding down with the issue of labels. This is something I hope we can talk about more during the question-and-answer period. Labeling is the essence of politics in a society that is media dominated. One of the most loaded among those labels is "terrorism." The *New York Times*, which has an institutional bias against the Salvadoran guerrillas, often refers to what they do as

141

terrorism in news stories without any sourcing. You can look in Wednesday's *New York Times* and find the phrase "terrorism" attached to what the Salvadoran guerrillas do. As we pointed out to the *New York Times*, we have never once in six years of Nicaraguan contra atrocities against civilians seen the term "terrorism" used in application to the Nicaraguan contras, and I would say that is a stark discrepancy. When the *New York Times* covered contra atrocities, the euphemisms could always be found in the lead and the headline. Stephen Kinser once turned in a story about how the contras had killed a government co-op leader and nine other civilians, several of whom were children. This was the *New York Times'* headline: "A Day's Toll Shows Contras' Ability to Strike." Remember what I said earlier about us laughing to keep from crying? The *New York Times'* headlines can often keep us laughing. They tend to put the best face on their allies or people in power. I remember once, around the summit, they had an article that quoted [Margaret] Thatcher's views on Reagan, and the quote had Thatcher saying, in the middle of the article, "Poor dear, there's nothing between the ears." And the headline was, "Thatcher Salute to the Reagan Years."

Now to get back to Central American labels. You always hear the dichotomy, "Nicaragua and its four democratic neighbors." The *New York Times* writes in that way. I do not think I have to go into details about what's not objective, neutral, or accurate about that. In Nicaraguan prisons, around the time of the Arias accord, the detainees were referred to in the *New York Times* and elsewhere as "political prisoners." The people in Salvadoran prisons, what were they? Leftist guerrillas. We pointed out to the *New York Times* that we have met with a lot of these people behind bars [in El Salvador]. There were not that many of them but we had met with those who survived the death squads and executions. A lot of them were women who had never held a gun. We asked, how can you call them leftist guerrillas, especially when most of them have never had a trial? Then we got a change from the *New York Times*: "alleged" leftist guerrillas.

As to humanitarian aid to the contras, I do not think I have to go into what is wrong with that, but I will if you are not sure. The Nicaraguan government has always gotten a prefix. It is an adjective: either "Marxist," "leftist," or "Marxist-Leninist." Almost never does the Salvadoran government get an adjective.

Like all baby boomers I do not want to finish this without talking about the instrument in our lives that we grew up with, and that is the television set. If you notice a narrow spectrum of sources that appear in print articles, you will also find on television a parallel phenomenon of a very narrow spectrum of opinion commentators, analysts that get on these shows. I think "MacNeil-Lehrer" has got one of the most overrated reputations for being somehow an alternative to the three major TV networks. Its spectrum of views is often very, very narrow. An example is a September 1987 news story that Nicaragua had reopened media outlets and declared certain cease-fire zones. PBS's "MacNeil-Lehrer" had three commentators on the story: (1) a Nicaraguan contra, (2) Elliott Abrams, who called it a "trick," and (3) Phyllis Oakley, of the State Department who said it was "cosmetic." I would argue that is not a fair spectrum. A couple of months later the show had an in-depth discussion of the peace process. This was the panel: on the right, Congressman Bob Dornan; in the center, Elliott Abrams; and on the left, Chris Dodd [Sen. Christopher J. Dodd (D-Conn.)]. I would argue that is two to one.

In February 1988, I am sure a lot of you activists and academics were following the major contra vote that was coming up. The night before the vote you must have watched "Nightline." What was the panel? Ted Koppel had his panel of four people: contra leader Alfredo Cesar, contra supplier [Retired Army] General [John] Singlaub, contra booster Robert Owen, and a Democratic congressman. Well, I mean, I grew up in America: fair was two against two and not three against one. Ted Koppel, by the way, has admitted his contra sympathies in an article in *Newsweek*. So, in a sense, it was three and one-half against one. FAIR has just completed a study of the "Nightline" guest list, beginning in January of 1985, and we found that the most frequent guests on that show during the period of our study were—are you sitting down?—yes: Henry Kissinger, Alexander Haig, Jerry Falwell, and Elliott Abrams. Now, I would argue that is not a fair spectrum even though—I do not know if Mr. Bendaña is still here—he is in the top ten. That is not a fair spectrum of views. I want to end laughing instead of crying as usual. There is one good thing about that list in terms of Alexander Haig in particular. You do not ever have to worry that Haig is one day going to barge into the studios of ABC's "Nightline" and announce, "I'm in control here." He apparently gets invited enough; he does not have to worry.

ABOUT THE EDITORS AND CONTRIBUTORS

The Editors

Sung Ho Kim is an associate professor of political science at Ohio University, where he teaches international relations, law, and organization. With a special research interest in the normative problems of international relations, Kim's publications include "The Issues of International Law, Morality, and Prudence," in *Reagan Versus the Sandinistas: The Undeclared War on Nicaragua*, edited by Thomas W. Walker (Boulder: Westview Press, 1987).

Thomas W. Walker is a professor of political science and director of Latin American studies at Ohio University. With a research interest in Nicaragua dating from his first visit there in 1967, he has authored, coauthored, or edited several books on that country or on Central America, including *Nicaragua: The Land of Sandino*, 3rd ed. (Boulder: Westview Press, 1991), *Understanding Central America*, with John Booth, 2nd ed. (Boulder: Westview Press, 1992), and *Revolution and Counterrevolution In Nicaragua* (coauthored, edited) (Boulder: Westview Press, 1991).

The Authors (as of 1988)

Manuel Rodríguez Arriaga. Mexican Deputy Secretary of Foreign Affairs for International Cooperation, Ambassador Rodriguez had been a key participant in his country's pivotal effort to promote peace in Central America since the birth of the Contadora process in 1983. Decorated by the governments of Argentina, Belgium, the Federal Republic of Germany, Brazil, France, Great Britain, Greece, Japan, Spain, Venezuela, and Yugoslavia, he was the Kennedy Lecture keynote speaker in the Central America symposium held at Ohio University in November 1988.

Alejandro Bendaña, who holds a Ph.D. in history from Harvard University, had worked in Nicaragua's diplomatic service from the time of the Sandinista victory in 1979. In addition to that of secretary-general of the Ministry of Foreign Affairs, he had also held the posts of Ambassador to the United Nations and director-general of Multilateral Affairs.

L. Francis Bouchey, president of the Council for Inter-American Security, Washington, D.C., is coauthor of the famous "Santa Fe document" of 1980, a conservative position paper which had been credited with having shaped the Latin American policy of the Reagan administration. He and the Committee of Santa Fe which produced the 1978 document have also released *Santa Fe II: A Strategy for Latin America in the Nineties* (Washington, D.C.: The Council for Inter-American Security, 1989).

Jeff Cohen, media critic, columnist, and lecturer, is the founder and executive director of FAIR (Fairness and Accuracy In Reporting), the New York-based media watch organization. His work at FAIR has won the praise of major journalism figures, such as Studs Terkel, I.F. Stone, and Ben Bagdikian. Cohen's columns have been published in dozens of leading dailies, including the *Los Angeles Times*, the *Boston Globe*, the *Atlanta Journal-Constitution*, the *Chicago Sun-Times*, and the *International Herald-Tribune*. He is regularly quoted about the media in publications such as the *New York Times*, the *Washington Post*, and *Newsweek*, and has discussed media issues on national TV and radio programs, including "ABC World News Tonight," "Nightline," CNN's "Crossfire," "Larry King Live," and C-SPAN.

William Goodfellow. Director of the Center for International Policy in Washington, D.C., Mr. Goodfellow had traveled frequently to Central America, where he had been deeply involved in covering the peace process since the early days of the Contadora initiative. In addition to numerous articles on that subject authored or coauthored in the Center's *International Policy Report*, he has also published Op-Ed pieces in a number of this country's leading daily newspapers.

Fred Kiel. As United Press International news director for Mexico and Central America, Mr. Kiel had coordinated all UPI coverage of Central America since 1982. Having worked in the isthmus as a stringer for the

Washington Post, the *San Francisco Chronicle*, and the *Miami Herald* from 1976 to 1978, he moved to the UPI Foreign Desk in New York where he served as editor for Central American and Mexican news until assuming the position as news director.

Walter LaFeber. Noll Professor of American History at Cornell University, Dr. LaFeber is the author, coauthor, or editor of more than a dozen books, including *The Panama Canal: The Crisis in Historical Perspective* (New York: Oxford University Press, 1978), and *Inevitable Revolutions: The United States in Central America* (New York: W.W. Norton, 1984), which was awarded the Gustavus Myers prize in 1985.

Carolyn J. Lukensmeyer. The first woman to serve as chief of staff of an Ohio governor, Dr. Lukensmeyer holds a Ph.D. in organizational behavior from Case Western Reserve University in Cleveland. She had worked as an organizational consultant and traveled widely in Latin America. Appointed in 1986, she served Governor Richard Celeste during the period in which he attempted to block the Reagan Administration's sending of Ohio National Guardsmen to "train" in Honduras.

Howard J. Wiarda. Professor of political science at the University of Massachusetts, research associate for the Center for International Affairs at Harvard University, and adjunct scholar of the American Enterprise Institute in Washington, D.C., Dr. Wiarda is author, co-author, or editor of a score of books on Latin America including *The Communist Challenge in the Caribbean and Central America* (Washington: American Enterprise Institute, 1987), *Rift and Revolution: The Central American Imbroglio* (Washington: American Enterprise Institute, 1984), and his widely used college text, *Latin American Politics and Development* (with Harvey F. Kline), 3rd ed. (Boulder: Westview Press, 1990).

Robert Witajewski. Country officer for Nicaragua in the Bureau of Inter-American Affairs of the United States Department of State, Mr. Witajewski received his B.A. and M.A. degrees in political science from the Universities of Michigan and California at Berkeley, respectively. Before assumimg his position as Nicaragua desk officer, he had tours of duty in Venezuela (1981-1983) and Guatemala (1983-1985) and in the Executive Secretariat in Washington (1985-1987).

MONOGRAPHS IN INTERNATIONAL STUDIES

ISBN Prefix 0-89680-
Africa Series

36. Fadiman, Jeffrey A. *The Moment of Conquest: Meru, Kenya, 1907.* 1979. 70pp.
     081-4 $ 5.50*

37. Wright, Donald R. *Oral Traditions From the Gambia: Volume I, Mandinka Griots.* 1979. 176pp.
     083-0 $15.00*

38. Wright, Donald R. *Oral Traditions From the Gambia: Volume II, Family Elders.* 1980. 200pp.
     084-9 $15.00*

41. Lindfors, Bernth. *Mazungumzo: Interviews with East African Writers, Publishers, Editors, and Scholars.* 1981. 179pp.
     108-X $13.00*

43. Harik, Elsa M. and Donald G. Schilling. *The Politics of Education in Colonial Algeria and Kenya.* 1984. 102pp.
     117-9 $12.50*

44. Smith, Daniel R. *The Influence of the Fabian Colonial Bureau on the Independence Movement in Tanganyika.* 1985. x, 98pp.
     125-X $11.00*

45. Keto, C. Tsehloane. *American-South African Relations 1784-1980: Review and Select Bibliography.* 1985. 159pp.
     128-4 $11.00*

46. Burness, Don, and Mary-Lou Burness, eds. *Wanasema: Conversations with African Writers*. 1985. 95pp.
129-2 $11.00*

47. Switzer, Les. *Media and Dependency in South Africa: A Case Study of the Press and the Ciskei "Homeland."* 1985. 80pp.
130-6 $10.00*

48. Heggoy, Alf Andrew. *The French Conquest of Algiers, 1830: An Algerian Oral Tradition*. 1986. 101pp.
131-4 $11.00*

49. Hart, Ursula Kingsmill. *Two Ladies of Colonial Algeria: The Lives and Times of Aurelie Picard and Isabelle Eberhardt*. 1987. 156pp.
143-8 $11.00*

50. Voeltz, Richard A. *German Colonialism and the South West Africa Company, 1894-1914*. 1988. 143pp.
146-2 $12.00*

51. Clayton, Anthony, and David Killingray. *Khaki and Blue: Military and Police in British Colonial Africa*. 1989. 235pp.
147-0 $18.00*

52. Northrup, David. *Beyond the Bend in the River: African Labor in Eastern Zaire, 1864-1940*. 1988. 195pp.
151-9 $15.00*

53. Makinde, M. Akin. *African Philosophy, Culture, and Traditional Medicine*. 1988. 175pp.
152-7 $13.00*

54. Parson, Jack ed. *Succession to High Office in Botswana. Three Case Studies*. 1990. 443pp.
157-8 $20.00*

55. Burness, Don. *A Horse of White Clouds*. 1989. 193pp.
158-6 $12.00*

56.   Staudinger, Paul. *In the Heart of the Hausa States.* Tr. by
        Johanna Moody. 1990. 2 vols. 653pp.
        160-8 $35.00*

57.   Sikainga, Ahmad Alawad. *The Western Bahr Al-Ghazal Under
        British Rule: 1898-1956.* 1991. 183pp.
        161-6 $15.00*

58.   Wilson, Louis E. *The Krobo People of Ghana to 1892: A
        Political and Social History.* 1991. 254pp.
        164-0 $20.00*

59.   du Toit, Brian M. *Cannabis, Alcohol, and the South African
        Student: Adolescent Drug Use 1974-1985.* 1991. 166pp.
        166-7 $17.00*

60.   Falola, Toyin, ed. *The Political Economy of Health in Africa.*
        1992. 254pp.
        168-3 $17.00*

61.   Kiros, Tedros. *Moral Philosophy and Development: The Human
        Condition in Africa.* 1992. 178pp.
        171-3 $18.00*

Latin America Series

8.   Clayton, Lawrence A. *Caulkers and Carpenters in a New World:
        The Shipyards of Colonial Guayaquil.* 1980. 189pp, illus.
        103-9 $15.00*

9.   Tata, Robert J. *Structural Changes in Puerto Rico's Economy:
        1947-1976.* 1981. xiv, 104pp.
        107-1 $12.00*

11.   O'Shaughnessy, Laura N., and Louis H. Serra. *Church and
        Revolution in Nicaragua.* 1986. 118pp.
        126-8 $12.00*

12.   Wallace, Brian. *Ownership and Development: A comparison of
        Domestic and Foreign Investment in Colombian Manufacturing.*
        1987. 186pp.
        145-4 $10.00*

13. Henderson, James D. *Conservative Thought in Latin America: The Ideas of Laureano Gomez.* 1988. 150pp.
    148-9 $13.00*

14. Summ, G. Harvey, and Tom Kelly. *The Good Neighbors: America, Panama, and the 1977 Canal Treaties.* 1988. 135pp.
    149-7 $13.00*

15. Peritore, Patrick. *Socialism, Communism, and Liberation Theology in Brazil: An Opinion Survey Using Q-Methodology.* 1990. 245pp.
    156-X $15.00*

16. Alexander, Robert J. *Juscelino Kubitschek and the Development of Brazil.* 1991. 429pp.
    163-2 $25.00*

17. Mijeski, Kenneth J., ed. *The Nicaraguan Constitution of 1987: English Translation and Commentary.* 1990. 355pp.
    165-9 $25.00*

18. Finnegan, Pamela May. *The Tension of Paradox: José Donoso's The Obscene Bird of Night as Spiritual Exercises.* 1992. 179pp.
    169-1 $14.00*

19. Sung Ho Kim and Thomas W. Walker, eds., *Perspectives on War and Peace in Central America.* 1992. 150pp.
    172-1 $14.00*

Southeast Asia Series

31. Nash, Manning. *Peasant Citizens: Politics, Religion, and Modernization in Kelantan, Malaysia.* 1974. 181pp.
    018-0 $12.00*

38. Bailey, Connor. *Broker, Mediator, Patron, and Kinsman: An Historical Analysis of Key Leadership Roles in a Rural Malaysian District.* 1976. 79pp.
    024-5 $ 8.00*

44. Collier, William L., et al. *Income, Employment and Food Systems in Javanese Coastal Villages.* 1977. 160pp.
031-8 $10.00*

45. Chew, Sock Foon and MacDougall, John A. *Forever Plural: The Perception and Practice of Inter-Communal Marriage in Singapore.* 1977. 61pp.
030-X $ 8.00*

47. Wessing, Robert. *Cosmology and Social Behavior in a West Javanese Settlement.* 1978. 200pp.
072-5 $12.00*

48. Willer, Thomas F., ed. *Southeast Asian References in the British Parliamentary Papers, 1801-1972/73: An Index.* 1978. 110pp.
033-4 $ 8.50*

49. Durrenberger, E. Paul. *Agricultural Production and Household Budgets in a Shan Peasant Village in Northwestern Thailand: A Quantitative Description.* 1978. 142pp.
071-7 $10.00*

50. Echauz, Robustiano. *Sketches of the Island of Negros.* 1978. 174pp.
070-9 $12.00*

51. Krannich, Ronald L. *Mayors and Managers in Thailand: The Struggle for Political Life in Administrative Settings.* 1978. 139pp.
073-3 $11.00*

56A. Duiker, William J. *Vietnam Since the Fall of Saigon.* Updated edition. 1989. 383pp.
162-4 $17.00*

59. Foster, Brian L. *Commerce and Ethnic Differences: The Case of the Mons in Thailand.* 1982. x, 93pp.
112-8 $10.00*

60. Frederick, William H., and John H. McGlynn. *Reflections on Rebellion: Stories from the Indonesian Upheavals of 1948 and 1965.* 1983. vi, 168pp.
111-X $ 9.00*

61. Cady, John F. *Contacts With Burma, 1935-1949: A Personal Account.* 1983. x, 117pp.
114-4 $ 9.00*

63. Carstens, Sharon, ed. *Cultural Identity in Northern Peninsular Malaysia.* 1986. 91pp.
116-0 $ 9.00*

64. Dardjowidjojo, Soenjono. *Vocabulary Building in Indonesian: An Advanced Reader.* 1984. xviii, 256pp.
118-7 $26.00*

65. Errington, J. Joseph. *Language and Social Change in Java: Linguistic reflexes of Modernization in a Traditional Royal Polity.* 1985. xiv, 211pp.
120-9 $20.00*

66. Binh, Tran Tu. *The Red Earth: A Vietnamese Memoir of Life on a Colonial Rubber Plantation.* Tr. by John Spragens. Ed. by David Marr. 1985. xii, 98pp.
119-5 $11.00*

68. Syukri, Ibrahim. *History of the Malay Kingdom of Patani.* Tr. by Connor Bailey and John N. Miksic. 1985. xix, 113pp.
123-3 $12.00*

69. Keeler, Ward. *Javanese: A Cultural Approach.* 1984. xxxvi, 564pp.
121-7 $25.00*

70. Wilson, Constance M., and Lucien M. Hanks. *Burma-Thailand Frontier Over Sixteen Decades: Three Descriptive Documents.* 1985. x, 128pp.
124-1 $11.00*

71. Thomas, Lynn L., and Franz von Benda-Beckmann, eds. *Change and Continuity in Minangkabau: Local, Regional, and Historical Perspectives on West Sumatra.* 1986. 363pp.
127-6 $16.00*

72. Reid, Anthony, and Oki Akira, eds. *The Japanese Experience in Indonesia: Selected Memoirs of 1942-1945.* 1986. 411pp., 20 illus.
132-2 $20.00*

73. Smirenskaia, Zhanna D. *Peasants in Asia: Social Consciousness and Social Struggle.* Tr. by Michael J. Buckley. 1987. 248pp.
134-9 $14.00*

74. McArthur, M.S.H. *Report on Brunei in 1904.* Ed. by A.V.M. Horton. 1987. 304pp.
135-7 $15.00*

75. Lockard, Craig Alan. *From Kampung to City. A Social History of Kuching Malaysia 1820-1970.* 1987. 311pp.
136-5 $16.00*

76. McGinn, Richard. *Studies in Austronesian Linguistics.* 1988. 492pp.
137-3 $20.00*

77. Muego, Benjamin N. *Spectator Society: The Philippines Under Martial Rule.* 1988. 232pp.
138-1 $15.00*

78. Chew, Sock Foon. *Ethnicity and Nationality in Singapore.* 1987. 229pp.
139-X $12.50*

79. Walton, Susan Pratt. *Mode in Javanese Music.* 1987. 279pp.
144-6 $15.00*

80. Nguyen Anh Tuan. *South Vietnam Trial and Experience: A Challenge for Development.* 1987. 482pp.
141-1 $18.00*

81. Van der Veur, Paul W., ed. *Toward a Glorious Indonesia: Reminiscences and Observations of Dr. Soetomo.* 1987. 367pp.
142-X $16.00*

82. Spores, John C. *Running Amok: An Historical Inquiry.* 1988. 190pp.
140-3 $14.00

83. Tan Malaka. *From Jail to Jail.* Tr. and ed. by Helen Jarvis. 1990. 3 vols. 1,226pp.
150-0 $55.00*

84. Devas, Nick. *Financing Local Government in Indonesia.* 1989. 344pp.
153-5 $16.00*

85. Suryadinata, Leo. *Military Ascendancy and Political Culture: A Study of Indonesia's Golkar.* 1989. 250pp.
179-9 $18.00*

86. Williams, Michael. *Communism, Religion, and Revolt in Banten.* 1990. 356pp.
155-1 $16.00*

87. Hudak, Thomas John. *The Indigenization of Pali Meters in Thai Poetry.* 1990. 237pp.
159-4 $15.00*

88. Lay, Ma Ma. *Not Out of Hate: A Novel of Burma.* Tr. by Margaret Aung-Thwin. Ed. by William Frederick. 1991. 222pp.
167-5 $20.00*

ORDERING INFORMATION

Orders for titles in the Monographs in International Studies series may be placed through the Ohio University Press, Scott Quadrangle, Athens, Ohio 45701-2979 or through any local bookstore. Individuals should remit payment by check, VISA, MasterCard, or American Express. People ordering from the United Kingdom, Continental Europe, the Middle East, and Africa should order through Academic and University Publishers Group, 1 Gower Street, London WC1E, England. Orders from the Pacific Region, Asia, Australia, and New Zealand should be sent to East-West Export Books, c/o the University of Hawaii Press, 2840 Kolowalu Street, Honolulu, Hawaii 96822, USA.

Other individuals ordering from outside of the U.S. should remit in U.S. funds to the Ohio University Press either by International Money Order or by a check drawn on a U.S. bank. Most out-of-print titles may be ordered from University Microfilms, Inc., 300 North Zeeb Road, Ann Arbor, Michigan 48106, USA.

Prices do not include shipping charges and are subject to change without notice.